Why Choose
the Liberal Arts?

MARK WILLIAM ROCHE

Why Choose the Liberal Arts?

University of Notre Dame Press

Notre Dame, Indiana

Reprinted in 2012

Cover: Paul Klee, *Highway and by-ways* (*Hauptweg und Nebenwege*), 1929,
90, oil on canvas, 83.7 x 67.5 cm, Museum Ludwig, Köln (ML 76/3253).
© 2010 Artists Rights Society (ARS), New York / VG Bild-Kunst, Bonn.
Reproduced by permission of Artists Rights Society. Image courtesy of
Rheinisches Bildarchiv, Köln.

Library of Congress Cataloging-in-Publication Data

Roche, Mark William.
    Why choose the liberal arts? / Mark William Roche.
        p.   cm.
    Includes bibliographical references.
    ISBN-13: 978-0-268-04032-1 (pbk. : alk. paper)
    ISBN-10: 0-268-04032-X (pbk. : alk. paper)
    1. Education, Humanistic. I. Title.
LC1011.R63 2010
378'.012—dc22
                        2010028741

∞ *The paper in this book meets the guidelines for permanence and durability
of the Committee on Production Guidelines for Book Longevity of the Council
on Library Resources.*

With gratitude and thanks to

my mentors and colleagues at

Boston College High School,

Williams College,

the University of Tübingen,

Princeton University,

The Ohio State University,

and the University of Notre Dame.

Contents

Acknowledgments   ix

Introduction   1

1   Engaging the Great Questions   15

2   Cultivating Intellectual and Practical Virtues   51

3   Forming Character   101

4   Integrating the Values of the Liberal Arts   147

Notes   173

Works Cited   182

Acknowledgments

Although I completed this book after serving a long term as dean of the College of Arts and Letters at the University of Notre Dame, I was able to begin the manuscript while serving as dean, thanks to a partial leave during the spring of 2007, which was generously granted by Thomas G. Burish, provost, and Rev. John I. Jenkins, C.S.C., president.

I am grateful to a number of colleagues who offered helpful comments on a draft version of the book: Kathy Cunneen, Ted Fox, Vittorio Hösle, Katie Lehman, John McGreevy, Scott Moringiello, Don Potter, Gretchen Reydams-Schils, and Greg Sterling.

In addition, the final version benefited from comments made by students in my Spring 2008 senior seminar on "Great Questions and the Liberal Arts." In particular, the suggestions of Kristen Drahos, Jessica Nelson, and Michael Popejoy led to changes in the manuscript. Also one of my graduate students, Erik Larsen, was kind enough to offer helpful suggestions.

The manuscript was enriched by comments and questions from audiences at several colleges and universities, where I presented earlier versions of this manuscript: Baylor University, Furman University, Hope College, and Spalding University.

Finally, I gratefully acknowledge permission from the Association of American Colleges and Universities to include material from a short essay entitled "Should Faculty Members Teach Virtues and Values? That is the Wrong Question," which appeared in *Liberal Education* 95.3 (Summer 2009): 22–27.

Introduction

What can my child do with a major in philosophy? That is the kind of question I received as dean every year during Junior Parents Weekend. Such questions are important and deserve a well-rounded response. Parents want to know that their financial investment will help their sons and daughters secure a livelihood. Students themselves want to know that what they are doing fits into a larger plan.

But students and parents all too rarely receive adequate answers to such questions. University leaders are busy solving the daily onslaught of myriad problems and trying to satisfy unquenchable demands for new resources; as a result, reflection on the ultimate purpose of education often takes a back seat. When academic leaders do speak of the liberal arts, for example, at first-year orientation or at graduation, they may speak in an abstract way, divorced from the practical needs and questions of students and their parents.

Students who major in philosophy, or in anthropology or chemistry or art history, have chosen the liberal arts. They are experiencing broad and versatile learning, and they are immersed in a distinctive element of American higher education and a source of its great vitality. However, in an age of increasing specialization and ever greater emphasis on immediately practical goals, the number of students who choose this path has declined over the years, and a need has arisen to articulate the diverse values of the liberal arts. Not only administrators are silent. Faculty members, too, may neglect to speak with students about the broader value of a liberal arts education. Some are enmeshed in their own specific disciplines, with which they identify more than with the broader purpose of a college. To others, the value of a liberal arts education seems self-evident, but to students and families who are sacrificing time and money and are eager for a practical return on their investment, its value is not immediately apparent. As Carol Barker notes, "Students and families need help in understanding how the liberal arts contribute to personal development and career opportunity" (10).

A recent national survey revealed that "parents and college-bound high school students have very little familiarity with the meaning or purpose of the liberal arts" (Hersh, "Liberal" 31). Not surprisingly, in an environment where the value of a liberal arts education is no longer taken for granted, only a minority of undergraduate degrees are awarded in the liberal arts. In the United States today, almost 60 percent of undergraduate degrees are in pre-professional and technical fields, with business leading the way, accounting for some 21 percent of all degrees awarded.[1] In the early decades of the twentieth century, in contrast, pre-professional and technical majors accounted for fewer than 30 percent of the undergraduate degrees (Brint et al. 155–56). In response to this desire for more immediate relevance, some liberal arts colleges have created new programs in vocational areas to attract students (see Breneman; and, more recently, Baldwin and Baker). Of first-year students at colleges and universities across the United States, 73 percent identify "being very well off financially" as "essential" or "very important," a figure that has risen over the past decades from a low of 36 percent in 1970; it is now the highest value identified by students. Related, only 51 percent of first-year students consider "developing a meaningful philosophy of life" to be "essential" or "very important," down from a high of 86 percent in 1968, when it was the highest value.[2] In this context, it is perhaps not surprising that the 2006 report of the special commission on improving American higher education, appointed by then–U.S. Secretary of Education Margaret Spellings, does not even mention the phrases "liberal arts" or "liberal education."[3]

The focus on "practical" pursuits may be even stronger in developing countries, where many new institutions of higher learning offer curricula only in those subjects perceived to be practical, such as business, science, or technology, a common practice in China, or where governments award scholarships primarily to students who are pursuing practical disciplines, such as engineering, science, and technology, as is the case in Uganda.[4] As might be expected, the most popular fields of study for foreign students coming to the United States are, first, business and management, and second, engineering (*Open Doors*).

In 2006 I traveled to Asia for several weeks with a group of university administrators and professors. In addition to getting a better understanding of Asia and meeting with alumni groups and Catholic Church leaders, we wanted to develop new research partnerships and enhance study abroad opportunities for University of Notre Dame students. One morning we took a tour of a higher education park in Suzhou, outside Shanghai, China. We began in the welcome center, which had on display a model of the park. A guide discussed one impressive venture after another, most of them focused on independent technology programs or cooperative arrangements with American and European universities in the fields of science and technology. I asked if they had any humanities programs. "Oh yes," said the guide, "we have several M.B.A. programs." As we walked further around the center, I noticed a photograph of two young women jumping high in the air. The caption read in English, "Flappy

Youth." I asked one of the Chinese professors from Notre Dame what she made of the caption. The term was related to the flapping of birds' wings, she said, and, after briefly reflecting, proposed instead "Soaring Youth." We passed the suggestion along to the guide, who insisted that the original translation had been done by the best translator in the area. It occurred to me, as impressive as their achievements in business, science, and technology might be, maybe they should teach more humanities.

In the United States, the better the students' high school academic records, the more likely they are to pursue the liberal arts (Brint et al.). Many of the nation's most selective liberal arts colleges and research universities offer majors only in the arts and sciences. Ironically, a recent study revealed that "liberal arts experiences and a liberal arts emphasis were most important for students of color and students with below average precollege academic ability."[5] In other words, although students with the highest academic standing are more likely to pursue a liberal arts education, the impact of such an education is even greater for students who are likely to have experienced disadvantages or who have below-average academic standing.

Both in developing countries and among first-generation college students in the United States, we often encounter a tendency to focus on practical, often economic and technological, needs at the expense of a wider palette of needs, desires, and capabilities, including those associated with broader intellectual enrichment and a fuller sense of well being. This is understandable, deriving from a hunger for basic subsistence and security, but when this focus inhibits a broader concept of human flourishing, it can be disadvantageous. Social scientists and philosophers have developed more nuanced understandings of human development and human progress beyond the Gross Domestic Product, or GDP, such as the Human Development Index, which takes into account life expectancy, literacy, and educational attainment, and the Genuine Progress Indicator, which accounts for the costs of ecological destruction, crime, and divorce. Such attempts, influenced by Amartya Sen's pioneering work on human capabilities, remind us that development is more than simply an account of economic and technological progress; true development is related to what people are able to do and be and so is deeply connected to values, to emotions, imagination, thought, and play, and to long-term human flourishing.

———

What are the "liberal arts"? The term has its origin in the medieval concept of the *artes liberalis*, the seven liberal arts that were appropriate for a free man (the Latin "liber" means "free") in contrast to the *artes illiberalis* or *artes mechanicae*, which were pursued for economic purposes and involved vocational and practical arts, which prepared young persons to become weavers, blacksmiths, farmers, hunters, navigators, soldiers, or doctors. The seven liberal arts included three basic arts focused on developing a felicity with language: grammar (or language), rhetoric (or oratory), and dialectic (or logic). These were known as the *trivium*. Added to these were the four advanced mathematical-physical arts: geometry, arithmetic, music, and astronomy, which were known as the *quadrivium*. Any Notre Dame student who passes through the Great Hall of O'Shaughnessy Hall, a space devoted to the elevation of the mind toward the transcendent, will find these seven original arts visualized in the set of seven stained glass windows. The liberal arts were preparatory not for gaining a livelihood but for the further study of law, medicine, and theology. Today, we understand the liberal arts to include the study of the arts and sciences, and we contrast the liberal arts with vocational education.[6]

In a contemporary liberal arts education, in contrast to the specialized orientation of professional or technical curricula, students receive a general education that is a broad grounding in the diverse disciplines. In addition to a wide distribution of courses, often with a core curriculum, liberal arts students major in an arts and sciences discipline, such as biology, history, or psychology, not in a professional or applied field, such as agriculture, criminal justice, or journalism. The exploration of a major provides depth and focus within the context of broader study, and this breadth aids specialized pursuits, as the more broadly educated we are, the better we are able to place new and specialized knowledge within a larger mosaic and to ask creative questions within our discipline from a range of alternative perspectives.

Beyond this curricular orientation and its high academic expectations, the liberal arts ideal entails the goal of educating the whole person, which presupposes a meaningful community of learning and a rich residential life experience. Its success demands intensive intellectual dialogue among students and between students and faculty across the diverse spheres of human inquiry and concerning the highest of human values. The formal dimensions of discussion and active student engagement are as much distinguishing characteristics of a liberal arts education as is the curricular content.

The liberal arts build on one of the oldest ideals of learning, which Socrates put into practice in ancient Greece. For Socrates it was clear that we learn more effectively when we pursue questions ourselves and seek the answers ourselves, when we embody what educators today call "active learning." The student is actively engaged in the learning process, asking questions, being asked questions, pursuing often elusive answers in dialogue with others. Knowledge cannot simply be poured, like water, from one larger container into an emptier one (*Symposium* 175d). Socrates also made it clear that learning is most important and most successful when students are engaged in meaningful discussions, asking questions that will determine who they are and what they think about life's most significant issues. For example, what is human excellence? What is friendship? love? courage? How do we learn? What constitutes the just state? It is not by chance that the questions in Plato's Socratic dialogues often have life-or-death consequences, as in the question that forms the center of the *Euthyphro*: What is piety?

A third pedagogical principle for Socrates, beyond active learning and meaningful learning, is that the Socratic method of engaging great issues through a question-and-answer format prepares the inquirer for further learning. This is one of the reasons why Plato's dialogues rarely offer answers, leaving the reader with an understanding of what she knows and doesn't know and the imperative to continue the path of inquiry on her own. To know something is not simply to mimic the truth but to be able to give reasons and arguments for that truth; this level of reflection ensures that the student will be able to defend a view against the arguments of future opponents instead of simply succumbing to their persuasive rhetoric; will be ready to apply knowledge in changing circumstances; and will be equipped to build on existing knowledge and extend it, via the same principles of searching inquiry and rational reflection, into new areas.

The modern classical writers on education—Montaigne, Locke, Rousseau, and Kant—all recognized these guiding principles. To educate, as in the Latin *educare*, means to lead out, to bring out from within. In his essays on education, Montaigne counsels that the student not simply listen and receive wisdom, based on authority, but instead grasp the value of doubting, learn to own knowledge independently, and be able to apply it in new and unexpected contexts; for that reason the student should avoid passivity: "We know how to say. 'This is what Cicero said'; 'This is morality for Plato'; 'These are the *ipsissima verba* of Aristotle.' But what have *we* got to say? What judgments do *we* make? What are *we* doing? A parrot could talk as well as we do" (154; bk. I, ch. 25). Locke elevates the student's presentation of her own ideas and her engagement in back-and-forth discussions with the teacher, which leaves "livelier, and more lasting Impressions" than silently and sleepily listening to lectures (§98). With Rousseau, the matter is even more pronounced, as active learning and existential engagement are among the overriding principles of his pedagogy. Although one can easily criticize Rousseau for his views on education, ranging from his naïve optimism to the impracticality of many of his ideas, he stressed throughout *Emile* that we learn more when we are actively engaged in the learning process (instead of simply receiving answers). He also emphasized that when topics have existential importance for learners, that is, when students see a connection between the ideas and the questions that animate them as persons, they learn more effectively.[7] In addition, Rousseau recognized "the desire to learn" (117) and the "faculty to acquire learning" (207) as being among the highest values of education. Kant, too, elevated the idea that the learner should be actively engaged in the process of discovering meaningful truths: "One learns most thoroughly and retains best that which one learns, so to speak, from oneself" (12: 736). For Kant, to be educated, indeed to be enlightened and free, is to have developed one's own capacity for reason and to be willing to use it "without direction from another": "Sapere Aude! [Dare to know!] Have courage to use your *own* understanding! That is the motto of the Enlightenment" (11: 53).

The idea that students learn more when they are themselves existentially engaged and active in the learning process, when they themselves generate their own questions, has been substantiated by recent empirical studies. Liberal arts students are frequently engaged in those activities that involve student-centered learning, such as small discussion classes, seminar papers, discussions outside of class with peers, service learning, study abroad, and independent research projects, including senior theses (Kuh, "Built" 126–30). Indeed, many innovations in undergraduate learning, such as first-year seminars, honors programs, and senior theses, were pioneered at liberal arts colleges (Rudolph 230–32, 237, 240–42). Other modes of fostering active learning in the liberal arts include essay examinations, oral examinations, and tutorials. Liberal arts students also tend to receive extensive feedback on their advancement toward learning goals. Empirical research makes clear that when students actively participate in the learning process, when they connect what they are learning to what they already know and find meaningful, and when they engage faculty outside the classroom on substantive topics, they learn more deeply and fully, and they enjoy the college experience more. One scholar sums up the matter concisely: "The greater the student's degree of involvement, the greater the learning and personal development."[8]

A liberal arts education is most pronounced, and most prominently realized, at small residential liberal arts colleges. Such colleges offer a broad general curriculum as well as majors in the arts and sciences. They offer extensive extracurricular activities in an intimate and nurturing environment. The campuses are often idyllic, classes tend to be small, and faculty devote themselves exclusively or almost exclusively to undergraduates. Campus populations are commonly fewer than 2,500 students. Liberal arts colleges include such institutions as Amherst, Bowdoin, Carleton, Pomona, Swarthmore, and Wellesley. Most of the residential liberal arts colleges, including all of the examples just noted, are private; however, public liberal arts colleges exist as well, such as New College of Florida and St. Mary's College of Maryland.

Despite the frequent and indeed appropriate association of a liberal arts education with residential liberal arts colleges, a liberal arts education can also take place, not in quite the same form, but still in substantial ways, in other settings: at large research universities that house honors colleges or that have rich traditions of residential life; at comprehensive colleges with a high percentage of professional majors but with considerable requirements in the arts and sciences; or even beyond college itself, among those who experience opportunities to discuss a wide range of substantive issues in a communal setting. To deny that moments of a liberal arts education can transcend the liberal arts college would be analogous to suggesting that research and the discovery of new knowledge occur only at so-called research universities, such as the University of California, Berkeley or the University of Michigan. Students in computing or business, architecture or engineering, nursing or education can in principle take courses in their majors or in the arts and sciences that give them elements of liberal learning. Noting their small classes, intensive faculty mentoring, and cultivation of intellectual curiosity and research skills, leaders of small colleges whose curricula no longer match the traditional liberal arts curriculum, but which offer instead more career-oriented majors such as business, criminal justice, or nursing may still see themselves as part of the liberal arts tradition (Glenn).

Even in graduate school, aspects of the liberal arts can resurface. Graduate students, for example, may be encouraged to explore broader questions, and a graduate program may foster a community of learning, such that not only academics, or future faculty members, are developed, but also intellectuals. Whereas academics have the skills to research specific questions within their disciplines and to convey to students the knowledge of their fields, intellectuals, broadly defined, pursue learning for its own sake and stretch well beyond their own disciplines in engaging the great questions.[9]

In this book, I consider three partly overlapping grounds for a liberal arts education: first, its intrinsic value, or the distinction of learning for its own sake, the sheer joy associated with exploring the life of the mind and asking the great questions that give meaning to life; second, the cultivation of those intellectual virtues that are requisite for success beyond the academy, a liberal arts education as preparation for a career; and third, character formation and the development of a sense of vocation, the connection to a higher purpose or calling. Exploration of these three values—the intrinsic, the practical, and the idealistic—constitute the first three chapters of the book. The values are interwoven with one another in often complex and subtle ways; my analysis concludes, therefore, with a fourth chapter that reflects on the integration of these values. In an effort to offer examples within the broader discussion, I address the study of literature as a recurring thread throughout my reflections, suggesting how the reading of literature has intrinsic value, how the interpretation of literature fosters intellectual virtues, and how the engagement with literature helps students develop a sense of meaning and purpose.[10] One could easily substitute any number of liberal arts disciplines for literature.

I present an ideal vision of a liberal arts education, focusing on what such an education can and should become.[11] Much of the popular literature on higher education has vigorously criticized our colleges and universities. Beginning with Allan Bloom's bestseller in the 1980s, *The Closing of the American Mind*, an unrelenting wave of critics has lamented the state of higher education, whether attacking it from the right for succumbing to political correctness or from the left for having adopted too much of a corporate model. Many of the voices raised against Bloom and others have justly countered that there never was a golden age of education and that there have always been contrarian voices, arguing for the inclusion of this or that course or this or that text in the canon. A lack of consensus on a common vision of education has been the norm in America. But neither a harsh critique without a compelling and workable positive vision nor a simple suggestion that our ideals have always been conflicted will inspire students to pursue a liberal arts degree when the more "practical" disciplines beckon. For that reason, I have tried to give a strong defense of the liberal arts ideal, while noting some of the challenges and struggles that necessarily take place as we seek to realize that ideal.

Why Choose the Liberal Arts? interlaces broad theoretical reflections with empirical studies of what liberal arts students learn and what prospects exist for them after graduation. An entirely different level of argument arises from my own experience. I have occasionally interwoven personal and anecdotal reflections, partly to illustrate individual points and partly to give greater life to my overarching reflections. My own experiences have spanned an unusual range within higher education. I received an undergraduate education at one of the nation's premier residential liberal arts colleges, Williams College in Williamstown, Massachusetts. I had the benefit of pursuing a graduate degree at the University of Tübingen in Germany, where I experienced a model of education radically different from any institution in the United States. My doctoral work was undertaken in the Ivy League, at Princeton University. Having experienced both small and large private universities, I spent the first twelve years of my career as a faculty member at one of the nation's largest public universities, The Ohio State University, serving as a chairperson for my last five years. In 2008, I completed my eleventh and final year as dean of the College of Arts and Letters at the University of Notre Dame, arguably the world's greatest Catholic university and a university with an unusually distinctive identity and ethos. Drawing on experiences in the course of more than thirty years in higher education, as a student, faculty member, and administrator, I can give further shape to some of the ideals and some of the frustrations associated with the vision and reality of a liberal arts education.

These reflections may interest undergraduates who major in the liberal arts, many of whom worry about their choice. Among such students, self-doubt and unease about life after college are not uncommon. *Why Choose the Liberal Arts?* also addresses the parents of liberal arts students, some of whom believe that their sons and daughters should instead major in something practical, such as business. It may also appeal to administrators who champion the liberal arts, as they seek to develop their own distinctive institutional vision. Faculty members teaching in the arts and sciences may find in these pages an evocation of one of their highest callings. Moreover, those who work in fields that are losing students and who worry about surrendering faculty positions might encounter strategies that could help them attract students to their courses. Students majoring in vocational and technical fields but who must take selected courses in the arts and sciences might, after reading this book, see in those general education requirements distinctive opportunities.

Part of learning is being motivated to learn; an articulation of possibilities and outcomes that are desirable can motivate students to learn better. A student in one of my recent senior seminars told me that he recognized the true value of college only as he was nearing graduation: in some ways, he wished he could start all over again, and this time go through college with greater awareness and more meaning. Perhaps such a volume can help students see the purpose of college at an earlier stage and thus help them make more of their time there. The need for such understanding has been recognized by others. A 2009 survey on *Trends and Emerging Practices in General Education* reveals that well over a third of institutions surveyed are placing increasing emphasis on "orientations to the purposes and value of liberal education" (9). Finally, while many businesses understand the value of hiring liberal arts graduates, many hire business majors and then lament that their new employees lack the most important quality they seek, communication skills. This trend has been documented for at least the past six years, with the most recent survey indicating that 50 percent of employers found their new hires to be lacking in communication skills (*Job Outlook* 15, 24). With a bit more awareness of what liberal arts graduates could do, businesses might avoid this unfortunate problem.

Hiring liberal arts graduates in business does not mean simply enhancing the communication skills of employees; it also involves having employees whose education has encouraged them to develop a moral compass and ask searching questions. In an age that has suffered tremendous financial crises—partly as a result of a failure of managers and leaders in business as well as in government to grasp the larger picture—the liberal arts are more essential than ever.

1

Engaging the
Great Questions

A liberal arts education can be defended first and
foremost as an end in itself; that is, it is of value for its own sake
independently of its preparing students for eventual employment. As an end in itself, a liberal arts education contrasts
strongly with the increasingly common notion, informed by the
credentialism and achievement ethos of our era, of education as
primarily a means to an end. Indeed, a recent study has shown
that "students and parents overwhelmingly believe the reason to
go to college is to prepare for a prosperous career" (Hersh, "Intentions" 20). In the wake of contemporary society's elevation
of *instrumental rationality* (how do I achieve a given end?), we
notice an increasing neglect of *value rationality* (which ends
should I pursue?). A liberal arts education asks questions about
those higher ends, those ultimate values. Not only does it help
us discover intrinsic goods, it is itself an intrinsic good. Liberal
arts students gain insight into what has supertemporal value,
they explore the challenges specific to our age, and they learn
to express wonder and awe. Becoming engaged with a range of

disciplines and questions is its own reward. A classic and compelling defense of this ideal of learning for its own sake was given by John Henry Cardinal Newman, who argued that "there is a knowledge worth possessing for what it is, and not merely for what it does" (86). Newman states further that "there is a Knowledge, which is desirable, though nothing come of it, as being of itself a treasure, and a sufficient remuneration of years of labour" (86).

Through the liberal arts, students explore profound and evocative questions, engaging issues that appeal to their curiosity and desire for knowledge and deepening the restless urge to see how ideas fit together and relate to life. Great questions naturally form themselves in the minds of young persons. I once spent a day exploring great questions with a group of advanced high school students in Germany. The conversation was part of an endeavor, undertaken by German philosophers, to understand what deep questions animate young persons. When I asked the students what philosophical questions most engaged them, they named quite a few, but two sets of questions dominated. The first set circled around God. After my original concept of God as an old man with a beard, sitting above a cloud, has been shattered, can I still believe in God? Is there a concept of God that is compatible with reason? And if a more mature concept of God is possible, what would it look like? Such searching questions are almost inevitable for young persons who have been raised in a religion and then encounter, for any number of reasons, doubts about their earlier, more naive concepts of God. The second set of questions revealed an innate interest in the natural world and a fascination with the place of the individual within the almost unfathomable vastness of the universe: Does space end, or is it infinite? Has time always existed, or was there a beginning? If there was a beginning, what existed beforehand, and if time has existed forever, how did we ever get to the present moment?

Those were not their only questions. They also wanted to know: What are the defining characteristics of our age and our generation? What virtues are most needed today? Why is there evil, and why must innocent persons suffer? What is the meaning of death? Are mathematical truths something we invent, or are they somehow already present, simply waiting to be discovered? How do we know that there are normative truths? Are there philosophical concepts that can help us in our conflicts with our parents and with others? Do we possess free will, or is everything determined? Questions such as these are often met with unease by parents. The questions are complex, and meaningful answers are not easy. Also, our broader society lacks a rich culture of conversation that would embrace, rather than cast aside, such questions. But complex questions such as these are essential to a deeper understanding of the world and of ourselves.

Even as students bring great questions with them to college, the university cultivates in them a curiosity about questions they had yet to consider: Why are there wars? What is the highest good? Is it better to suffer or to commit an injustice? What are the best conditions for human flourishing? What are the defining characteristics of the just state, and how might we most effectively change our state to approximate that ideal? What are the great artworks of the ages? How do planets form, and how did life on earth arise? Is there, or was there ever, life elsewhere? Why is there anything at all, and why not nothing? Do science and religion necessarily conflict? What were the great turning points in history? Why do some countries develop successfully and others stagnate? What are our generation's most pressing moral obligations? Which, if any, of the world's religions are true? Do animals have consciousness? How does the mind work? None of these questions permit simple answers, and they do not all have practical value in the truncated way in which we tend to define practical value, but they do *matter* to students. To understand our world as it is and to understand our world as it should be are values in and of themselves.

━━━━━

What do students explore in the individual disciplines of the arts and sciences? In mathematics, students study patterns, both empirical and imagined. They learn how to explore numbers and shapes, to develop mathematical proofs, and to perform differentiation and integration, which are essential for measuring motion and change. They become familiar with the fundamentals of probability and randomness, learn methods of statistical analysis, and become astute evaluators of quantitative evidence. Through their study of logic, they advance their capacity for clear thinking, and in their exploration of both rigorous theory and wide-ranging applications, they begin to see in mathematics a discipline of beauty and wonder.

Students obtain through the natural sciences a richer comprehension of the world. They learn to observe natural phenomena with a keen and inquisitive eye. They gain an understanding of the universe, its evolution and structure; the fundamental laws and phenomena that underlie both physical and biological systems; the natural history of our planet, solar system, and galaxy; the composition and properties of elemental forms of matter; and the principles governing the activities of living systems in relationship to their environments. They learn to apply reason to evidence, to form concepts that relate to experience, and to induce laws from the sequence of phenomena. They develop a hunger for data, and they learn to test their theories against reality and to see in reality beauty and grandeur. In addition, they grasp the ways in which scientific principles and insights help to inform important issues of public policy and human welfare, and they become adept at assessing arguments that are based on scientific claims.

In psychology, students explore the human mind. They study the ways in which both biology and environment influence thought and behavior. They explore the development of the human being, from infancy to old age. They examine questions of perception, cognition, memory, and learning as well as decision making and problem solving. They develop and assess theories of personality and of interpersonal relationships, and they analyze individual and collective identity crises. They seek to understand, prevent, and alleviate mental health problems and to know the conditions necessary for human flourishing.

Through their study of the social sciences, students learn to analyze and appreciate the diverse ways in which social and political structures are organized. They achieve a greater awareness of the common and distinct characteristics of peoples and cultures. They study human development across time and cultures, cultivating a richer sense of the motives, attitudes, and values that animate individuals and societies. They explore the ways in which social structures influence human behavior. They devise categories for understanding the complex relationships, including the economic forces, that shape our world, and they learn to approach problems and questions with formal and statistical models. They investigate forms of conflict and power as well as diverse styles of leadership. They study the varied impact of scientific and technological change. They learn how to sift and evaluate the wealth of information and competing claims that crowd us on a daily basis, and they learn how to apply quantitative and qualitative methodologies to help analyze and solve complex problems.

Through the study of history, students cultivate an appreciation of diverse contexts and traditions, a sense of the complexity of causal forces as well as of the great debates of the ages and the dialectic of continuity and change. They learn what is involved in the analysis and interpretation of the past, including the sifting of a wide variety of documents and the close study of pertinent materials. They develop an empathy for and an appreciation of what is different. They learn to understand how contemporary challenges relate to, and derive from, earlier developments, and through their knowledge of other eras, they gain a wider horizon and thus a richer perspective on contemporary challenges.

An experience of the arts, which appeals to our imagination, emotions, and intellect, makes visible to us the multiple riches of the senses and enables students to grow in self-awareness, creativity, and sensitivity. Through their exploration of the arts, students gain a greater understanding of nonverbal communication. The arts help students recognize the gap between the world as it is and the world as it ought to be while at the same time reconciling them to what is good and beautiful about the world they have inherited. Art assists the individual's search for edification and contributes to the collective identity of a culture. Indeed, art offers a window not only onto the collective identity of a given culture but also onto the complexity and dignity of humankind and indeed onto the transcendent itself. Participation in art gives students all of these qualities as well as experience in both disciplined collaboration and creative innovation.

The study of language and literature cultivates in students verbal precision as well as a sensitivity to language and its potential for complexity and elegance. It provides them with an awareness of rhetoric and style. It educates them to think more imaginatively, to see the world through metaphors and stories. The reading of literature gives students an appreciation for form, an understanding of, and empathy with, a wide range of human experience, and a nuanced grasp of hermeneutics, or the art of interpretation. It also alerts them to the persuasive and manipulative power of language. The study of other languages and literatures offers students encounters with the diversity and magnificence of human expression and affords them new insights into their own language and culture. It gives them experience with translation as well as a greater social sensibility and an awareness of another culture's history and civilization. In addition, it allows students to communicate with others across linguistic and cultural boundaries.

The study of religion offers students insight into religious artifacts, rituals, and texts and engages them in the complex interplay of faith and reason and the search for religious wisdom. At its depth, the study of religion is not only disinterested, allowing for objective exploration of the subtleties of religious practices and differences among religions, but also existential and formative, allowing students, within the paradigm of theology, to recognize a link between God and truth, to grow in understanding of the mysteries of their faith, and to experience a formation that speaks to the whole spirit oriented toward God in intellect and love.

Students of philosophy experience the joy of asking and exploring questions concerning the opportunities, obligations, and ultimate meaning of human life. They analyze methods of understanding reality as well as the processes and conditions of understanding itself. Philosophy gives students insight into the whole of knowledge and into the presuppositions and ends of the diverse disciplines. It teaches them how to justify correct positions and criticize false opinions, to uncover flaws in assumptions and arguments. It encourages them to relate all aspects of life to the principles of ethics. Beyond giving students tools for analysis and judgment, philosophy cultivates the love of wisdom and teaches them that thought is its own end.

Liberal arts students are encouraged to develop not only an awareness of knowledge intrinsic to their major but a recognition of that discipline's position within the larger mosaic of knowledge. The college or university citizen is invested in the search for not only specialized knowledge but also the relation of the diverse parts of knowledge to one another. To be liberally educated involves knowing the relative position of the little that one knows within the whole of knowledge (Hösle, "Great Books"). Mathematics helps us see the basic structures and complex patterns of the universe, and the sciences help us understand and analyze the laws that animate the natural world, the inner world, and the social world. History opens a window onto the development of the natural and social worlds. The intellectual fruits of art and literature, the wisdom of religion, and the ultimate questions of philosophy illuminate for us the world as it should be. In essence, then, the arts and sciences explore the world as it is and the world as it should be. While not every class at every college helps students grasp the higher principles articulated above, the ideal liberal arts classroom does more than focus on specialized questions and teach technical knowledge; it relates those specific pursuits to the overarching purpose of a discipline and of intellectual query in general. An ideal liberal arts experience also ensures that students are familiar with the questions raised in disciplines beyond their own major or concentration.

A goal of every university is to explore the unity of knowledge across disciplines. A legitimate concern that arises when developing countries move away from the concept of the university and instead create focused institutions of business and engineering is the loss of this unity of knowledge, even as a regulative ideal. Wisdom is the ability to understand and interpret individual phenomena from the perspective of the whole. An institution of higher education that does not include diverse disciplines or a theory of learning that brackets overarching or ultimate questions is not well suited to the cultivation of wisdom, which is no less necessary to address the challenges of our age than are particular technical skills.

One of the greatest joys of serving as dean was gaining an understanding of a full array of disciplines beyond my own. Each time a department was evaluated, each time a promotion and tenure case was reviewed, each time a potential faculty member was interviewed, an opportunity arose to learn about the recent developments in and the most engaging questions of a given discipline. What are some of the most counter-intuitive insights ever discovered by psychologists? In what ways has economics evolved in recent years? What are the most pressing methodological debates in history? What are the most important unsolved problems in philosophy? Why should a student major in English? What are the best strategies for teaching painting? Each field contributes in fascinating ways to the full mosaic of knowledge. These arts and sciences disciplines differ from fields, such as architecture, business, engineering, law, and medicine, whose goals are associated less with knowledge for its own sake and more with knowledge as it is applied to activity in the world.

In some arts and sciences disciplines we recognize great historical progress; in others we develop extraordinary admiration for past achievements. Whereas science is almost always measured in terms of advancements, in the arts and humanities many peerless works derive from earlier eras. We do not today seek to understand the world via eighteenth-century biology, but we don't hesitate to read Plato and Sophocles, Dante and Goethe to engage in rich intellectual and aesthetic experiences and to understand the world better. Few would argue that such writers have somehow been superseded. The distinction between science as necessarily progressive and the arts and humanities as not participating in progress in quite the same way was one of the principal reasons for the historical separation of the arts and sciences in the seventeenth century (Kristeller 526). Some of the prerequisites for greatness in the arts and humanities—emotional richness, the cultivation of diverse virtues, breadth of knowledge, and formal mastery—may diminish through the ages. Certainly, within the arts and humanities we recognize the introduction of new forms and more contemporary themes. However, the greatness of a work is measured not simply by its formal innovation or the local currency of its theme.

This lack of progress is not necessarily to be lamented; on the contrary, it means that the past is alive. We are not alone in our age but can find enriching perspectives in the past, which thereby becomes very much a part of the present. We have reason to look toward other ages with great humility as we reflect on great works, whose forms embody their messages and in which the parts and whole reinforce one another in organic and inexhaustible meaning.

A humbling sense of the value of the past is essential for us as we recognize that not everything can be addressed via advances in instrumental or technical rationality. The balanced self requires not only rationality, analysis, and discipline, but also playfulness, sympathy, and beauty. Today, philosophical synthesis and reflection on eternal values have for the most part given way to specialization and utility. The pragmatic concept of truth as utility is intimately connected to the reign of instrumental reason, which usurps the traditional hierarchy of *theoria* (contemplation) and *poiesis* (production). In an era that elevates the act of making, we tend to neglect the value of contemplation and the leisure that makes it possible. The British philosopher Bernard Bosanquet captures the concept well, writing that "leisure" was for the Greeks

> the expression of the highest moments of the mind. It was not labor; far less was it recreation. It was that employment of the mind in which by great thoughts, by art and poetry which lift us above ourselves, by the highest exertion of the intelligence, as we should add, by religion, we obtain occasionally a sense of something that cannot be taken from us, a real oneness and centre in the universe; and which makes us feel that whatever happens to the present form of our little ephemeral personality, life is yet worth living because it has a real and sensible contact with something of eternal value. (1: 488)

For the early Christians this ancient concept still held sway and became in their eyes *otium sanctum*, or sacred leisure. Augustine writes: "the love of truth seeks sacred leisure" (*City of God* XIX.19, translation modified).

In modernity leisure seems to disappear. Technical inventions and eventually social techniques increase the pace of life. With technology the world moves more quickly. Not by chance Tommaso Campanella's seventeenth-century utopia *City of the Sun* concludes with a description of a new invention followed by the lack of time to continue more leisurely discussion. Dialogue is not all that is threatened. From television screens in waiting rooms to cell phones, iPods, and BlackBerries on the streets, meaningful solitude, which allows us to gain distance from the distractions and cliches of the age, is threatened. Already in the seventeenth century, Pascal took note of the range of human distractions and the hesitancy to spend quiet time with one's own thoughts (e.g., 70, 165, 168, 515); the developments of technology only exacerbate this universal temptation.

Contemporary society has little patience for the apparent idleness of learning for its own sake. Today we elevate an instrumental form of thinking, a means-end rationality, in ways that tend to obscure what is of intrinsic value. Ironically, means-end thinking does not lead to happiness or well being. Happiness is not something that can be bought, purchased, sought; it comes to one with meaningful values as a gift. In addition, the elements of spontaneity and vitality, play and tranquility, which also belong to happiness, are neglected to the very extent that instrumental reason is elevated. Moreover, when reflection on how to reach certain ends becomes supreme, it easily overshadows the question, which ends should I seek to achieve.

In "The Organization Kid," David Brooks underscores the ways in which contemporary students view college as a full schedule of industrious activities and a means toward further advancement. Rightly understood, however, a liberal arts education is more than a means to an end; it is a dose of *otium* (leisure) in a world driven by speed and utility. To devote one's time to exploring the great questions is not to negotiate the automatic rungs of the ladder of success, but to step out, pause, and deliberate. The origin of the word "school" or Latin "scola" derives from the Greek term for leisure (*scholē*). This is not leisure in the sense that most Americans think of leisure. It represents the values of rest and focus in advance of, as a respite from, and as a reward for, daily work, and it is analogous to repose and silence as presuppositions for meaningful communication with God. When we are gripped by substantive works and great questions, we may be so immersed in them that we forget the external world. We lose ourselves in what we are reading and thinking. Through the leisure of contemplation we abandon the contingent and engage the eternal; we conceive of ourselves as more than merely material beings. Such joy does not, and need not, serve a purpose beyond itself. If we believe Aristotle, we do not rest primarily in order to work more effectively; on the contrary, the business of work serves the external purpose of giving us the conditions for leisure and repose, on which the joy of contemplation, our highest end, depends (*Nicomachean Ethics* X.7).

The Paul Klee oil painting I chose for the cover of this book conveys, I think, a suggestion of what we might understand by the ordered and energetic leisure of a liberal arts experience. Klee paints a magically alluring canvas of diverse and interesting paths. The soft light of Klee's painting receives a certain vibrancy from the dominance of two colors at opposite ends of the color wheel, orange and blue. Inspired by a southern landscape, the painting is nonetheless mediated, abstract, reflective. The painting has been officially rendered by the Paul Klee Foundation as "Highway and by-ways" (*Paul Klee* 5: 297), but a more literal translation of *Hauptweg und Nebenwege* would be "Main Path and Side Paths." Whereas highway connotes a busy road, the German *Weg* implies a more leisurely, pedestrian path. A path (or way) is of course not simply a topographic marker but a metaphor for the journey of a human life, a life path. Klee's painting evokes a colorful but cerebral mosaic of an ordered main path enriched by more freely drawn side paths, on which one can also meander and which help to form the pattern of one's life journey. The main path brings us forward, but the various side paths do not detract from our journey; on the contrary, they enrich and help to constitute it. In studying such a painting, not unlike experiencing the liberal arts, we are invited to meander freely and reflectively over many colorful paths, which form a complex, contemplative pattern and which lead upward to an open and inviting horizon.

In our age, consumerism and pleonasty, the bondage of worldly things, tend to distract us from the heights of contemplation. One of the dominant goals of modernity has been to increase living standards and consumption; both of these factors have contributed to the definition of social success. As Arnold Gehlen notes in *Man in the Age of Technology*, anyone with historical consciousness cannot help but recognize that earlier generations had a much different view of ascetic values: "In any case the individual who renounced the goods of this earth always enjoyed a moral authority, whereas today he would be met with incomprehension" (78, translation modified). Asceticism, according to Gehlen, "adds to the integration and composure of the personality, and at the same time sharpens the social impulses and increases spiritual awareness" (106, translation modified). One need only think of Augustine's elevation of fasting as resistance to the temptations of the world—sensual pleasures, shallow curiosity, and wealth—that draw us away from our highest values or of Aristotle's and Aquinas's arguments that the contemplative person is more self-sufficient, closer to the divine, engaged in what is most distinctive about human beings, and more removed from our common preoccupation with externals.[1] What is distinctive about human beings is thought, love of wisdom, and love of one another in the contemplation of highest values, including goodness. An engagement with great questions and a love of thought allow all external trappings to recede in importance.

Ancient wisdom, the precursor of the liberal arts ideal, recommends less immersion in the instrumental so that we can devote ourselves more fully to the enjoyment of what is already available: contemplation, dialogue, friendship, the exploration of nature, and the experience of beauty. We see in this ancient wisdom an elevation of the intrinsic over the instrumental. The idea extends from the ancients to the medieval Christian ideal of contemplating divine truth. Augustine, for example, suggests that "contemplation is promised us as the end of all activities and the eternal perfection of all joys," and Aquinas argues that the "essence of happiness consists in an act of the intellect" and "in the contemplation of Divine things."[2] Modern human beings are hardly happier than their premodern predecessors, and persons in developed countries cannot be said to exhibit greater happiness than those in developing countries. Indeed, emotional poverty and depression are greater challenges in developed countries than in developing countries. This puzzle may underscore the wisdom in the often forgotten idea that to satisfy merely material needs is, beyond a minimal level and in the end, not our most meaningful or highest goal.

Indeed, the college experience is for most people a once-in-a-lifetime opportunity to engage great works, ask deep questions, foster one's identity, develop relations with peers, and pursue overarching principles for the most part unhampered by the distractions of material needs and practical applications. Anthony Kronman notes that "college is a time to explore the meaning of life with an openness that becomes harder to preserve the further one enters into the responsibilities of adulthood, with their many entanglements" (*Education's End* 40). In the years and decades after college, the number of external demands experienced by graduates increases and those who long for a rich intellectual life often lament the lack of time to pursue it (Katchadourian and Boli 279). Colleges seek not simply to please but also to educate, fostering an ethos that privileges the life of the mind and encouraging students to develop an identity by focusing on what is most essential. I can recall several occasions in college—whether it was working on an essay that fascinated me, going for an outing with friends, or spending a day with fellow students and a faculty member—when I intentionally placed my watch in my pocket to ensure that I was not distracted by time, by thoughts of what I needed to do otherwise or next. The symbolism of that gesture reinforced in me the value of complete focus, and many of those times remain among my most memorable. Only rarely is an adult able to recapture that level of freedom.

The isolation and almost otherworldliness of campus life serve a positive purpose. To garner through engagement with the great questions a sense of the world as it should be, we need distance from the world as it is. College, with its focus not on the everyday, but on the transcendent, its engagement as much with the past as the present, its consideration as much of the other as of the here-and-now, is an oasis of difference. The identity of the college student and the identity of a college as an institution are not reducible to serving the immediate needs and tendencies of the age. The liberal arts student has the capacity, removed from the everyday world and detached from primarily materialist or realist pursuits, to assess that world, not with the lens of someone immersed in it and already committed to this or that cause, but with the perspective of someone disinterested, who can bring to the world a different and transcendent standard, who can examine what is in the light of what should be, in the light of truth and justice and not in the light of particular and embedded interests.

In accord with this view, liberal arts educators do not always cater to student preferences. For example, setting up television screens in every common room on campus, such that quiet spaces for study and discussion are difficult for students to find, would be incompatible with the higher purpose of college. The goal of seeking knowledge for its own sake also serves the purpose of helping students see the world differently from those immersed in the categories of the age; it helps students see the world as it might and should be. The countercultural nature of a college education, its cultivation of knowledge and meaning for its own sake, is not a weakness, but the very strength of a college, for it offers students a vision of life that is contrary to what is already given to them and all around them. I do not mean to suggest that colleges are mistaken in engaging their surrounding communities or that students should be discouraged from performing welcome community service. On the contrary, I rejoice in these connections. I do, however, mean that colleges should proudly see themselves as countercultural in their elevation of questions that transcend the currency of the age; the engagement with such questions is one of their richest, if most undervalued, contributions to society.

Universities are a privileged space for thinking that is not immediately utilitarian but which in the end may have tremendous value; this long-range perspective is one of their most central missions and should not be truncated by external pressures for immediacy. Science must be given room for non-goal-oriented breakthroughs, which are often unpredictable. Pure science often has ripple effects that are discerned only over time, when a given application becomes apparent. To tie science and mathematics down to goal-oriented applications would be to reduce their potential for broader impact in the long run.

Moreover, colleges must continue to recognize the centrality of those disciplines, such as the arts and humanities, that will never generate significant external dollars but which are among the best poised to ask some of our deepest questions. These fields can create a space for the pursuit of topics that transcend a short-term payoff. Unfortunately, the autonomy of universities today runs up against what David Hollinger has aptly described as "the force fields of capital, where profit functions like gravity, where knowledge takes the form of property, where human energy is converted into money, and where values dance to the sound of markets" (80). Colleges that value learning for its own sake must forcefully communicate that an institution that preserves the great questions serves society in a way that is different from, but no less valuable than, an institution that addresses a nation's economic needs. When a college is asked to give an account of itself, it tends to focus, not surprisingly, given the economic paradigm of our age, on its economic impact on the larger community. A great college offers its graduates and its surrounding community more than the potential for greater income. By articulating that it offers more, it elevates the rhetoric of society, helping others to see that we are often beholden to mere means rather than to our highest ends. A campus that serves as a locus of meditation and serenity embodies and awakens this distinctive dimension of college life.

———

To study in order to engage the great questions and not simply to make a living is to raise our ambitions for what college might be. Often our ambitions simply are not lofty enough. There is a natural, human tendency to grab low-hanging fruit. If I can get by with a major in business and get a job, why not? After all, students in business consistently spend fewer hours studying than majors in the arts and sciences.[3] Moreover, at some institutions the decision by students to major in business frees them from requirements that are more common in the arts and sciences disciplines, such as advanced work in a foreign language.

Even faculty succumb to low ambitions, choosing at times not to take risks with their classes but instead offering well-tried classes that they know have worked well in the past. Also, some faculty produce trickles of scholarship, so as to receive a decent raise or to be promoted, but do not desire to change their discipline or to write a work that will be read fifty years from now. Low ambitions are also manifest in the increasingly narrow areas of specialization that many of us carve out for ourselves. Not surprisingly, Stanley Fish, who has argued against doing anything more than instructing students in the formal tools of one's discipline, titles one of his polemics against the lofty rhetoric of educators "Aim Low." Tocqueville analyzed the problem of ambition in his account of democracy in America, writing that all Americans are ambitious, but in small and petty ways, seeking "property, reputation, and power," but everyday Americans lack, he argued, "lofty ambition" (627). Tocqueville continues, "For the most part life is spent in eagerly coveting small prizes within reach" (629). Some pursue nothing but "vulgar pleasures" and "paltry desires," and he encourages us to project a higher idea of ourselves and of humanity (632).

One challenge to engaging the great questions are some of the trends and faculty proclivities at colleges and universities. The more specialized faculty members become in their research, the less likely it is that they will want to teach well beyond their area of expertise or to reflect on the higher purpose of their discipline. Many have themselves not experienced or no longer experience the intrinsic value of learning. Not all academics, as I have suggested, are intellectuals; that is, not everyone who teaches at a university is interested in more than solving limited problems. The ambition to tackle a great project in research or in teaching is not always frequent. This lack of ambition is not unrelated to a lack of confidence in measures of what constitutes a great work or even a great question. Further, the increasing unease with the concept of a great work has in the humanities led to considerable focus, in research and in teaching, on works that cannot easily claim to inspire the attention of students. Without a measure for greatness, many mediocre intellectual products have made their way into the halls of our colleges and universities. If the liberal arts attract students because of great texts and great questions, to the extent that faculty members substitute mediocre books that derive from faculty research interests or ideological perspectives, then student interest and passion will diminish.

This is not to say that great authors are not taught. They are, contrary to the image in the conservative media. However, it is to suggest that the range of works taught is much broader now than ever before, and texts are sometimes justified for inclusion in a syllabus not because students will find them meaningful but because they satisfy the often less than persuasive interests of faculty members. A faculty member whose own research was not on great works once told me that he thought that students would find great works too difficult, so he decided in all seriousness that he would instead teach "pretty good" books, which he viewed as a kind of technical term. Tocqueville would have been amused.

The very architecture of a college campus can foster the lofty ambitions we seek in students, just as it can nurture the sense of community and collegiality that is essential to good public discussion. When I arrived at Williams College as a first-year student, my dorm room, which I shared with two others, overlooked a set of stairs that led to West College, the oldest building on campus. Coming from someone who should be cynical after having served more than fifteen years in academic administration, it will sound idealistic and sentimental, but I still recall that I was deeply moved, indeed inspired, as a young man, seeking to develop my identity and thinking that college would be full of not only hard work but also lofty treasures, when I first read the words on the columns of Hopkins Gate, which frames the stairway to West College and which I passed every day of my first year: "Climb high / climb far / your goal / the sky / your aim / the star." I was similarly inspired and intimidated by the names of the great writers engraved high on the facade of Stetson Hall, some of whom I had read, but others were just names to me: Homer, Dante, Cervantes, Molière, Goethe, and so forth. These were implicit signals to me about what mattered. I had so much still to learn.

When I was a graduate student in Tübingen, I was captivated by the idea that the university was celebrating its five-hundred-year anniversary. The same cobblestone streets and alleys that I walked were also the paths of Hegel and Hölder-lin and Schelling, all great writers I was studying. At Princeton there was a distinctive room in East Pyne Hall, layered with beautiful woodwork, from floor to ceiling, and filled with books. When the famous German writer Martin Walser entered the room, he elegantly said, "Hier lernt man von selbst." The expression, which cannot be gracefully translated, conveys the idea that in such a space one learns almost by osmosis. The very size of Ohio State conveyed to me a seriousness about leaning; all of these resources and buildings, stretching further than the eye could see, were devoted to the ideals of learning and scholarship. The Golden Dome, which shines beautifully on the Notre Dame campus, similarly conveys an ennobling sentiment to faculty, staff, and students whose minds are looking for inspiration and higher aspirations. The layout of the campus itself, which takes the shape of a cross, echoes this sense of transcendent purpose.

Students benefit from every available form of assistance, as the wider culture does not tend to elevate the minds of young persons. In his 2007 commencement address at Stanford University, Dana Gioia, at the time Chairman of the National Endowment for the Arts, argued that higher education should offer students an opportunity to pass beyond "the easy comforts of entertainment" to "the challenging pleasures of art."[4] The comment could be extended more broadly: college is about great questions that students can learn to love, but like all great ambitions, it requires a passion for lofty aspirations and a willingness to engage in hard, yet rewarding, work. College is indeed a different kind of leisure.

━━━

Our experience of art and literature differs from the routine experience of consumption and utility. When we appreciate an object of beauty, we do not desire to possess or transform it, to consume or use it; we leave it free as it is. Our experience of literature is of value for its own sake. It is "purposeless" in the higher sense of being its own end. When we read lesser works, we tend to focus solely, or at least primarily, on the information we take from them, reading such works for practical purposes. The experience of great literature differs: relevant here is the personal experience of reading, including the affective response triggered by a work's sensuous structures and components, which are not reducible to what we carry away from a work on the level of information. The experience of reading great literature is defined by intense concentration of attention, a lingering over the complexity of formal structures, patience in exegesis, a love of continuing mystery. I can still remember reading Dostoevsky's deep and complex *Brothers Karamazov* on my sister's bed (she had moved out and her room had the best light in the house) in the summer before my senior year of high school; reading Thomas Mann's ambitious and gripping novel *Doctor Faustus* partly on the train in Germany, partly on a park bench in Tübingen; and reading Adalbert Stifter's richly ambiguous and moving tale *Abdias* while on a long flight across the Atlantic. Each of these works opened another world for me, whether it involved the various ways in which we long for ultimate knowledge, what is at stake when a character is tempted by evil, or how human aspiration and the possibility of redemption conflict with fate. Others will have analogously fond recollections of gripping reading experiences.

An engagement with great literature is its own reward, an experience of value in and of itself. In this sense it is higher than many values we elevate on a regular basis, yet which are themselves mere means to other values. Making money is both necessary and useful, but it is *merely* useful, undertaken for the sake of something else, whereas the joy of contemplation is an end in itself, an activity pursued for its own sake. The goods of the spirit do not have their end beyond themselves, in some other entity; they thus contrast with so-called useful endeavors, which, however, are useful only insofar as they serve other ends.

What is most useful, Brand Blanshard suggests paradoxically, is what is valued as an end in itself, that is, what is often passed off as useless: instead of helping us reach some higher goal, it is itself a most worthy goal (32). Josef Pieper argues that "there are certain things one cannot do 'in order to . . .' do something else. Either one does not do them at all, or one does them because they are meaningful in themselves" (58, translation modified).

Consider within this context the connection between the intrinsic value of reading great literature and the self-sufficiency and richness of play. Play is a childlike, but nonetheless meaningful, activity in which we experience, in a free and voluntary way, the intrinsic joy of engaging our faculties, including our imagination. Johan Huizinga argues in his classic study of this subject that, along with reason and making, play is central to our being. He thus proposes *homo ludens* (playing man) as complementary to the more popular *homo sapiens* (knowing man) and *homo faber* (working man). Play serves many hidden purposes: it allows us to rejoice in vital inclinations; it engages and expands the imagination; it conjures up a temporary world of order and beauty; it provides balance to the more instrumental and ordinary sphere of work through its disinterested and extraordinary dimensions; it proffers new modes of seeing and relating; and it offers us an experience of ritual. This elevation of leisure and play in the context of wisdom is vibrant not only in the Hellenic but also in the Judeo-Christian tradition, as is evident from passages such as Proverbs 8:30–31, where Wisdom plays before God and delights God; Sirach 38:24–25, which suggests that the wisdom of the learned person depends on the opportunity of leisure; or Luke 10:38–42, where Christ elevates Mary's love of wisdom over Martha's action and service.

In modernity, the theological paradigm, with its turn toward the transcendent, was increasingly displaced by the economic paradigm and its focus on the material and practical world. Although modernity, in glorifying work, action, and power, associated leisure with idleness, and play with indolence, the eighteenth-century German writer Friedrich Schiller resisted this tendency to disparage mere play. He counters, "The agreeable, the good, the perfect, with these a person is *merely* serious; but with beauty he plays" (*Aesthetic Education* 105–7, translation modified). Schiller states more fully: "But how can we speak of *mere* play, when we know that it is precisely play and play *alone*, which of all our states and conditions is the one which makes us whole and unfolds both sides of our nature [that is, the rational and the sensuous] at once?" (*Aesthetic Education* 105, translation modified). Schiller adds, "A person only plays when he is in the fullest sense of the word a human being, and *he is only fully a human being when he plays*" (*Aesthetic Education* 107). Play is done for its own sake, as an end in itself, and yet this experience enriches, it does not impoverish. Play may also be a means to an end, but that is incidental; it is primarily an end in itself, and as such, it becomes a means to an end—it enriches our sense of the value of what is done for its own sake. A liberal arts education is infused with this element of intrinsic value.

It is important that students with a liberal arts education be able to earn a livelihood. Parents want their children to succeed, to have a job that ensures shelter and puts food on the table. However, the utility of a liberal arts education cannot be reduced to its materialist dimensions. The great questions and the intrinsic value of learning, the element of play, give us categories for meaning and self-worth that counter a self-worth defined by what one has.

———

Answers to our searching questions are of interest whether or not they apply to the practical world. They satisfy an innate human longing for knowledge, indeed for wisdom. Yet not only the answers we discover, but also the simple pursuit of profound questions has intrinsic value. To explore a fascinating question, independently of the results, is to engage and elevate the mind. The German Enlightenment writer G. E. Lessing once said, "If God held all truth in his right hand and the sole ever-lasting urge for truth in his left, with the result that I should for-ever and always err, and said to me, 'Choose,' I would humbly bow before his left hand and say, 'Father, grant me this. Pure truth is for you alone'" (13: 24). The search for truth, the en-gagement with different positions, the experience of learning more, develops our highest capacities. The possession of truth without a search would, according to Lessing, make us "quies-cent, lazy, arrogant," whereas the search for truth gives value and vitality to our humanity.[5]

Of course a search for truth without any prospect whatso-ever of recognizing what might be true, a belief that is not un-common in the humanities today, is as much a death knell for meaningful inquiry as is the dogmatic belief that all truth is in our hands. Without any prospect of truth, we all too easily fall into indolence (as our search will always be in vain) or arro-gance (if there is no objective truth, I am free to define truth as I see fit). There are truths we can discover, including, for example, the very value of the search for truth as well as various scientific insights and basic moral obligations, and there are others to-ward which we can only strive and which in their complexity and inexhaustability will always partially elude us.

Faculty are sometimes hesitant to address the great ques-tions with students, partly because in doing so, they are forced to move beyond their specialized competencies and become searchers themselves, and partly because they worry about the connection between great questions and delicate issues of moral values, but students are as interested in the questions and the in-finite pursuit of truth as they are in precise and final answers. W. Robert Connor rightly notes that what students need are "not answers, but vocabularies, metaphors, exempla, and modes of thought" that will help them develop the "confidence, depth, and clarity" to think the questions through for themselves (10). Not every activity that is an end in itself reaches an end, and as students become aware that the most fascinating questions have hardly been exhausted despite a long tradition of historical reflection, they are both inspired and humbled.

This sense of longing for more intellectual engagement is one reason why many outstanding undergraduates choose graduate study. As noted earlier, a liberal education need not be restricted to undergraduate learning. The emphasis on breadth, on student engagement, on close student-faculty interaction, and on discussion of the great ideas as well as the development of intellectuals, rather than simply academics, can also arise in graduate programs. In addition, intellectual community can be fostered at the graduate level as much as, or in some cases even more than, at the undergraduate level because of the smaller student cohort, because of the number of classes taken in common, because of the texts that are read together in preparation for examinations, and because of the opportunity to develop friendships that are fostered by not simply common experiences but common intellectual experiences. This cultivation of the liberal arts ideal can occur to some degree in disciplinary graduate programs, though not without some effort, given ever increasing, if understandable, trends toward specialization. Interdisciplinary graduate programs, such as those in cognitive science, environmental studies, history and philosophy of science, medieval studies, or literature, may offer greater opportunities for advanced liberal arts experiences.

At some colleges and universities, students are required to take a set of general education courses that satisfy requirements defined by ways of thinking that an educated person should have developed. These can be courses chosen from a menu of offerings in quantitative reasoning, social analysis, oral and written communication, cross-cultural awareness, ethical inquiry, and so forth. Instead of simply satisfying disciplinary requirements, students take courses that meet the learning goals and outcomes desired by their institution. At a liberal arts institution, one could also imagine a course whose primary goal would be to help students reflect on the value of education itself. Those graduates who are vocationally trained will find that the specific practices that they learned in school will change over time. Because they might not have learned to reflect on the relation of those practices to a larger whole, they will likely be at a disadvantage compared to those graduates for whom broader reflection was an integral part of their education.

The student who experiences the intrinsic value of education develops autonomy, whereas the student whose education serves only an external purpose—a remunerative position or external accolades and recognition for accomplishments—lacks that privileged element of freedom. Such a person becomes dependent on that purpose; value comes not from the internal delight of exploring the life of the mind and engaging meaningful questions but from external approbation and success in the world. In his inaugural address on the value of studying universal history, Schiller suggests that the student who studies merely to make a living is interested in truth only insofar as it can be converted into "gold, newspaper praise, princely favors" ("Was heißt" 751). The student, in contrast, who loves truth is not finished with knowledge when it has served its external purpose but instead takes joy in continual discovery. Moreover, the student who explores learning only for its immediate application has no capacity to draw on the principles that alone make possible its appropriate application. Liberal arts students experience truth as "invested with all its possibilities" (Whitehead 93), transforming knowledge into an intellectual and even poetic adventure, which can energize them for their entire lives. The liberal arts student whose education has been successful lives for ideas, for the life of the mind, in which ideas have no less value than things. Indeed, for such a person the comprehension and contemplation of ideas may be said to have ultimate value—also as the standard for how we should live. It is an ancient ideal, captured beautifully in Socrates' dictum that the unexamined life is not worth living (*Apology* 38a).

———

After students graduate from college, they continue to be fascinated by the power of ideas, the complexities of the world around them, and artworks that they encounter for the first time. The joy of thinking and the enthusiasm of exploring will not cease for the liberally educated person. The strategies that best assist graduates in their pursuit of such experiences beyond college are to provide them with a solid base of intensive learning for its own sake—their college years—and to ensure that they develop during those years a love of learning as an end in itself. One of the ironies of a liberal arts education is that, although it is an end in itself, it is never-ending, that is, it is a life-long process. The leisure of college, meaningfully structured, makes it more likely that future opportunities for leisure will be enriched by reading, visiting museums, attending performing arts events, asking deeper questions—in short, by activities that give meaning and add mystery to life. The liberal arts experience of the intrinsic value of knowledge allows us to be comfortable in our own company, in our own thoughts, which is a precondition of character and depth. John Dewey notes, "The dominant vocation of all human beings at all times is living—intellectual and moral growth" (310). College can give its graduates "sources of inner fortitude, self knowledge, and personal renewal" (*College Learning* 23). As the German writer Jean Paul suggests, "A learned person is never bored" (1: 685).

———

College presidents sometimes refer to their elevator pitch. In the thirty or so seconds that they might be in an elevator with another president, a donor, or a journalist, they must succinctly articulate the strengths of their institution and back up their claims with selective data. Over my eleven years as dean, I had a series of elevator conversations of a different kind. One of the laments of any dean is the lack of time to pursue scholarship. When I would finally get to the library, it was usually at the end of a day on semester break, and when I did manage to gather a stack of books, it was the time of year when restricted hours reigned, and on multiple such occasions the circulation desk was closed. The security guard had to fill out the withdrawal slips for me. I frequented the library regularly only in fulfilling my administrative duties as dean. At Notre Dame, the top floor of Hesburgh Library is the site of most of our university receptions. Access to that floor requires a special key, and student workers staff the elevators for special events. On such occasions, upon entering the elevator, I always asked the students what their favorite class was. Invariably, the answer was something like history or theology or film or politics. When I then asked them what their major was, they often answered that it was business. There was a disconnect between what they liked intellectually and what they chose as their major.

When I asked students why they were majoring in business, they often referred to parental pressure or, in a few cases, more subtly, they expressed the concern that since their parents had sacrificed to pay for their education, they felt inwardly obliged to major in something practical. When, in contrast, I asked students who had transferred from business to arts and letters why they did so, the most common answers were that they had become fascinated with a discipline in the liberal arts or that their vocational classes were too boring.

Toward the end of my first year at Notre Dame, I traveled to Innsbruck, Austria, and interviewed all of the participants in our study abroad program there to get a sense of what was working well and what we needed to change. One question I asked every student was, "What did you like most about your year in Innsbruck?" The answers were varied. For some, it was making great advances in the language. For one, it was understanding Austrian history in a way that she never could have in the United

States. For others, it was the relationship with a host family, or the beauty of the city and the surrounding landscape, or the location in the center of Europe and the opportunity to explore museums and other attractions throughout the continent. Of the twenty or so students in the program, there was only one business major. While the arts and letters students struggled with the question, unsure of what to elevate as most singular above other wonderful experiences, the business major responded, "Oh, that's easy. Being around all these arts and letters students. They're so interesting."

One factor working against the elevation of intrinsic value is the overriding competition principle that rules our age. I am a tremendous fan of competition and of markets and introduced an abundance of incentives, efficiencies, and differential adjustments when creating new initiatives and assessing departments and faculty members at Notre Dame, but there are some departments that must be supported even if they do not bring in sufficient numbers of students or dollars. There are some values for which we need to sacrifice the competition principle, for it, too, is after all only a means to greatness, and we must be watchful for victims along the way.

Because faculty are not impervious to the tremendous demands on them and because most of them want to succeed in both teaching and research, colleges should offer ample opportunities to help them develop meaningful teaching strategies that are not unduly time-consuming. During my first weeks as a Notre Dame faculty member, I enrolled in an effective workshop entitled "Teaching Well, Saving Time." While no substitute exists for time devoted to one-on-one advising of students, how faculty prepare for classes should be as efficient as possible.

The competition principle has affected salaries at universities, driving many prospective faculty members to more lucrative positions outside the academy or to more applied fields within it, such as business, engineering, and law. To attract great students into the arts and sciences, universities and colleges need to offer them a vision of engaging the great questions that compensates for the loss of income and external prestige. In a world driven by speed and measurable advances, it takes considerable imagination to win students over to the life of the mind and to questions that transcend our age. Not surprisingly, liberal arts colleges, which tend to foster faculty-student relations and active learning on the part of students, including undergraduate research, do very well in producing graduates who go on to receive Ph.D.'s. Data on recipients of doctoral degrees in the humanities as well as in the social and natural sciences show that the percentage of graduates of liberal arts colleges who receive doctorates is much higher than at research universities and at other universities.[6]

Because the economy is tight for academic positions in most fields, faculty must nurture interest in this path among their best students and also counsel caution. I can recall one of my history professors at Williams inviting me to his home one afternoon. He peppered me with questions about my interest in pursuing a Ph.D. Did I know that I would not be guaranteed a job? Did I know that professors work unbelievable hours and are still not assured of tenure? Did I know that I would be dependent on the jobs available in a given year and would not be able to live where I might otherwise choose? Did I know that I would earn much less as a faculty member than in other professions? When I responded that all of that was just fine, that I viewed graduate school as an extension of my liberal arts education, and that I was flexible in my needs and so forth, he stepped back and said, "OK, you can go." I was grateful for the lesson.

In certain contexts, our challenge to students needs to shift in the other direction. At some universities, the dominant achievement ethos sends the best humanities students on to investment banking and law school, and students do not consider the joys of the life of the mind. As parents, professors, and university administrators, we need to remind students of the intrinsic rewards that trump power and salary. At Notre Dame, every year some 17–19 percent of the graduates in the College of Arts and Letters, in their desire to serve God and their fellow persons, devote themselves to a year or more of full-time volunteer service. But it should not be overlooked that an academic vocation is another way to come closer to God, engaging not in practical service but in contemplation as an end in itself, which is the activity that most mirrors the divine.

Most faculty members chose their profession because of a love of learning or because of a professor who inspired them and a resulting desire to offer similar experiences to others. There are some professors who report that, as graduate students, they were initially driven more by the research ideal than by the teaching ideal. However, I have found that for many of them, in the early stages of their decision to opt for graduate school, a desire to teach is dominant, and then it often recedes, as they identify with the profession as it becomes defined for them. We would do well to remind faculty members of their intrinsic sense of vocation. When I taught graduate students at Ohio State, most of them wanted to teach at liberal arts colleges. They wanted to be in a smaller community where they could get to know their students. Most faculty members would have advised them to aspire to jobs at research universities. When my first doctoral student had multiple offers, including one from a Big Ten university and one from a liberal arts university, Wake Forest, and chose the latter, one of my colleagues shook her head in disbelief. I admired the decision.

———

A liberal arts college cultivates for faculty as well as for students the intrinsic value of learning. When I was a student at Williams, we took four courses each semester and a so-called Winter Study, an intensive study of one course during the month of January. Students were encouraged to take courses outside their primary areas of interest, to widen their horizons. I can recall taking courses in music and in creative writing. Faculty members were likewise encouraged to teach courses outside of their primary areas of expertise. Such stretching fostered the elements of curiosity and intrinsic interest that are central to the liberal arts.

Scholars at a liberal arts college have the opportunity to experience the intrinsic value of knowledge in a special way. The former president of a highly ranked liberal arts college who has also served in prominent leadership positions at two premier research universities once told me the following story. A scientist at his former liberal arts college was a superb researcher in every respect. The president asked the scientist, given his compelling research record, if he had ever considered moving on to a research university. "At a research university," the scientist said, "the pressure for funding is such that one has to be funded and, therefore, one has to do research in those areas where funding exists. At a liberal arts college, I have more freedom. I can do research on what I want, and if there happens to be funding in that area, then I apply for it." Another distinction of liberal arts colleges is their integrative dimension of scholarship, which tends to differ from more specialized disciplinary knowledge (Ruscio; Oakley, *Community* 155–56). Because smaller colleges have fewer faculty members, they must teach a wider range of topics, and because the communities are smaller, forging intellectual bonds with colleagues in other disciplinary areas tends to be easier. Finally, frequent contact with undergraduate students, who are themselves not specialized, as are graduate students, encourages broader questions, in teaching and subsequently in research.

What transcends the liberal arts years are not only the intellectual interests that are formed but also the friendships. Over time these become among our longest-lasting friendships. Aristotle famously said that the highest friendships are based not on mere pleasure or mutual utility but on shared values and an intrinsic appreciation of one another (*Nicomachean Ethics* VIII and IX). In the highest form of friendship, we cultivate in one another what is the highest potential of humanity and the highest activity of the soul, goodness and intelligence. Such friendships are ends in themselves. We experience a shared commitment to the good, to what transcends and elevates us. In these relationships we learn how to become better persons. The intrinsic value of college friendships arises out of a context of identity formation in connection with a sharing of discussion and thought, an engagement with the great questions, whose primary purpose is not utility but meaning.

This vertical elevation to the transcendent has the effect of strengthening horizontal bonds. One of the marks of a liberal education is that it enables lasting friendships to form over ideas. When graduates visit with college friends, they share thoughts about what they are reading and what they think about recent world events. They ask about each other's vocation and professional puzzles. The liberal arts offer a vocabulary that sustains a language of deep friendship.

Intellectual activity and creativity are fostered by social interaction and intellectual community, by the back-and-forth of thinking out loud and contesting one another's ideas (Collins). College graduates are not surprised to hear that "the strongest single source of influence on cognitive and affective development is the student's *peer group*" (Astin, "Involvement" 126). For this reason, a meaningful liberal arts education presupposes a vibrant "community of learning" (Oakley, *Community*). The best liberal arts courses foster friendships. They encourage students to contribute in class, to offer their own perspectives and experiences, to comment on each other's work. The challenge, which can be met partly by the mediating role of caring faculty members, is to help students see a connection between their learning and their friendships, so that friendships are not purely social, something alongside schoolwork, but interwoven with learning and ideas. Such friendships are formed less often via clubs or activities or parties than in the classroom and in informal discussions surrounding class. What students in their inner core desire are trusted friends with whom they can speak about issues that matter. Such friendships, like the education in which they develop, are defined by their intrinsic value. Friendship and love, including the love of wisdom, are of value for their own sake.

I can recall the many ways in which community was fostered while I was an undergraduate at Williams. On the very first day, every first-year student lined up to shake the president's hand; it meant something to me, as well as to my parents, that the president knew me, even if only in a formal and symbolic way. I went to college when the drinking age was still eighteen and binge drinking, while it existed, seemed rarer, not least of all because drinking was not forbidden. I admired the fact that Williams had eliminated fraternities ten years or so before I arrived on campus. The college retained the buildings, which were located on campus, and turned them into intimate residential halls. As a sophomore, I lived in one of these halls and was approached by a group of seniors who asked me if I wanted to contribute twenty dollars to buy a keg for the basement lounge. The rules were that no one drank more than one or two beers per day, and no one drank before ten o'clock in the evening. The purpose was not to get drunk, but to engage in meaningful discussion. The kegs would be replenished until the money ran out. I was impressed with the concept and turned over my money. The conversations ranged from new art movements in Düsseldorf, Germany to what kinds of majors the investment banks in New York City prefer. My twenty dollars lasted the entire year. I never knew if it was because we drank so little or because one of the wealthier students decided to contribute more.

The former fraternities had their own dining halls. Once a week we had a special meal, with tablecloths and candles, and we could invite faculty members, who often lived near campus. Twice a week we had German Table at lunch, and a small number of students ate with faculty members, as they sought to develop their language skills further. I was invited to the homes of faculty members and still remember those evenings quite vividly. Today, I do the same for my students, and I can tell from their comments and occasional letters that such events mean a great deal to them. Not least of all, these gatherings bring the students together and indirectly endorse student fellowship. At Notre Dame, we recently received a generous endowment to support such activities. Our Table Talk program reimburses faculty members for the costs of purchasing food for meals at their homes and for meal tickets in the student dining halls. Because these events transform the atmosphere in classes, the program will pay more if an evening at a faculty member's home takes place during the first half of the semester instead of at the end of the semester.

Faculty sometimes forget that a sense of community is essential to any flourishing intellectual pursuit. Community is as important to graduate students and faculty as it is to undergraduates. When I was applying to graduate school, I submitted my applications from Germany and so did not visit any of the campuses. Upon arriving at Princeton, I discovered that most of the other students in our class of seven had narrowed their choices the previous spring to Princeton and Yale. Several visited Yale and told the same story. At Yale, there was at the time, in contrast to Princeton, little sense of community among the students or between students and faculty members. As a result, each of my colleagues chose Princeton. When in the early 1990s we resolved at Ohio State to fly the top prospective graduate students to campus before they made their decisions, we found that the yield of accepted students who chose to come to Ohio State rose dramatically. We offered them a community of learning that they could visualize. In the penultimate year of my tenure as dean at Notre Dame, the department of theology received a yield of 91 percent against the best universities in the country, consistently winning in head-to-head competition with Chicago, Duke, Emory, Princeton, and Yale. The department was not only strong academically, but the coordinators of the different fields arranged for prospective students to visit faculty homes; surely, the students could imagine the supportive social and intellectual environment that would be conducive to meaningful discussions in their years as graduate students.

While faculty-student contact is important, student-student contact is even more meaningful. Peer interaction is often cultivated by administrators who know that learning is deepened when student conversations don't simply flow from residential hall patter but build on discussions in classes. Some colleges have found it successful, for example, to place students from the same hall in at least one first-year class together or to offer occasional classes in the residence halls. For a number of years, the Ohio State University has offered a one-credit course on a "big idea," which brings students of various disciplinary perspectives together with faculty members and members of the community to explore a topic. Examples have included evil, passion, war, cities, immigration, and values. One of the goals of the course is to help students take ideas seriously and become conversant on important topics across disciplines (Livingston).

Student-student engagement not only fosters the best learning; it mimics the pursuit of learning that will continue after college. One of the virtues of a liberal arts education is the way in which it awakens or deepens curiosity and wonder, which in turn fosters continued learning beyond college, learning that will come more from peers than from superiors. The desire to continue to learn is a practical value, as we will see below, but it is first and foremost a human quality that ensures that our being is enriched by the life of the mind. To ask great questions that give meaning to ourselves and others is joyful, and for most persons this joy is fostered more easily at college than at any other time in our lives. Not so much the answers given, or the information learned, but, as Locke stressed already centuries ago, the habit of learning and thinking is what matters most, and that habit is not simply an intellectual value but a life value and its own reward.[7]

2

Cultivating Intellectual and Practical Virtues

To elevate contemplation as the highest good is not to suggest that action has little value, for the possibility of contemplation requires resources obtained through action, and only the practical intellect can address problems, such as abject poverty, that challenge human dignity and awaken our sense of duty. Students are called away from the contemplative to the active life, from college to work, in order to address their most basic needs, to develop further through experience, to participate in shaping the world, and to aid in the welfare of others. It is, therefore, not only ironic but also appealing that the very education we elevate for its intrinsic value cultivates virtues that serve meaningful external ends and prepares students for the needs and challenges of practical life, even if that is not its primary purpose. Although instrumental values are not the highest values, they are necessary if the highest values are to be realized in society. In a knowledge economy, moreover, the traditional dichotomy between the liberal arts, which focus on knowing and have their ends in themselves, and the practical arts, which focus on action and utility, is not absolute.

The idea that something can be both a means and an end is complex but hardly contradictory. The concept was introduced already by Plato, who draws the distinction in the *Republic*, recognizing that "there is a kind of good which we would choose to possess not from desire for its aftereffects, but welcome it for its own sake" (II.357b). Joy is one such example.[1] Plato then argues that a number of goods satisfy both components: there is "a kind we love both for its own sake and for its consequences" (II.357c). As examples, Plato notes sight, health, understanding, and justice. The power of sight, for example, gives us immediate pleasure, but it allows us to do many other things, from undertaking crafts to reading texts. A liberal arts education also fulfills both moments: it is its own reward and superb preparation for the world of work. Let me turn, therefore, in this second chapter to the utility, the instrumental value, of a liberal arts education.

Even though I have elevated the intrinsic value of liberal learning, I disagree with writers who claim that "knowledge, *by definition*, can be correctly called liberal only to the extent that it *cannot* be shown to have direct practical uses" (Graber 8). One of the defining virtues of modernity is that knowledge is transformed into action. Goethe's Faust, the paradigmatic figure of modernity, revises the Gospel's "In the beginning was the Word." He translates the *logos* of John 1:1 as *die Tat*: "In the beginning was the Act" (1237). Although justice depends on an idea of how the world should be, to live in the world of ideas alone would be to abandon our moral obligation to make justice real.

■

A liberal arts education helps students develop formal virtues, such as the ability to listen, analyze, weigh evidence, and articulate a complex view. It assists students in sharpening their analytical and verbal skills and expanding their creativity. Familiar with the enduring achievements of diverse cultures, the liberal arts graduate is at home in a world of ideas. The abilities to communicate clearly, think critically, and solve complicated problems; the capacity to draw on a breadth of knowledge while patiently focusing on appropriate details; the savvy to appreciate difference, complexity, and ambiguity; and the desire to continue to learn are all fostered in the liberal arts setting.

Above all, the liberal arts develop in students a refined ability to speak and write. The ability to speak well is partly fostered in well-orchestrated discussion classes. With extensive formal feedback from faculty members and often from peers, students learn to participate meaningfully in the give-and-take of discussion, listening attentively and asking other students to clarify their points, articulating their own perspectives and offering evidence to support them, and asking good, searching questions that take discussions to higher levels.

A course I regularly teach at Notre Dame is the College Seminar. The seminar places an emphasis on discussion and other activities that help students develop their capacities for oral expression and intellectual agility, with no less than two-thirds of the grade based on oral performance. Because a person can't speak well without first having thought deeply, in my version of the course students must write approximately sixty pages. The students take a thirty-minute one-on-one midterm oral examination and a forty-five-minute one-on-one final oral examination; for each examination, the student receives a page of written comments, which I dictate immediately after we meet. For most students it is a wonderful learning opportunity. The students receive extensive feedback, totaling about five pages of single-spaced comments by the end of the semester; these range from praise for specific comments and diverse kinds of contributions to suggested strategies for improvement and the recommendation that they overcome their use of specific filler words, such as "like," "you know," or "um."

A very appealing innovation came from a student. At mid-semester each year, I ask students three questions about the class: What are the two or three most effective elements in helping you achieve the learning goals of the course? Can you suggest some changes for the remainder of the semester that would better help you learn? If the course has helped you learn to date, what is the nature of that learning? One student suggested that students should give feedback to one another. I liked the idea, and with some advance notice, I asked every student to offer a sentence of praise and a constructive suggestion for every other student in the class. I reviewed all of them and then reformulated the submissions, so that each student received a page of anonymous praise and a page of anonymous suggestions. I was fascinated by how insightful the peer comments were and how meaningful students found the combination of generous praise and diplomatic, but demanding, criticism from their peers. This wonderful exercise could be achieved only in the kind of small classes one finds in a liberal arts environment.

Student tendencies and proclivities sometimes prevent them from learning as much as they might. While the expectations of students are influenced to a great extent by societal values and by faculty members, who either spark or fail to spark student interest, students must themselves assume responsibility. Perhaps the more they realize that their own active engagement, their own efforts to seek out topics of meaning, and their own need for tough and detailed feedback will help them learn, the more ambitious they will become in each of these areas. On the first day of most of my discussion classes, I break the students into small groups of three or four and ask them to explore the following questions: What were the two or three dominant characteristics of the best group discussions they have ever had and what generated those successes? And what were the two or three characteristics of the worst discussion classes they ever had and how could those experiences have been avoided? After some animated conversation in the small groups, we get together as one body, and I list on the board what they have identified. I then assign responsibility for the success of our discussion classes either to me (for example, the selection of a fascinating topic and not dominating the discussion by lecturing to students) or to them (good preparation, a willingness to share ideas, a readiness to listen attentively to others, etc.). They are amazed at the extent to which they themselves are responsible for making a class either great or mediocre.

Of course, students will engage only if the topic is fascinating, the readings are engaging, and they know that their efforts will lead to meaningful learning. In some cases for students to learn, faculty must devote more time to setting up the course well and to motivating students and less time to imparting their knowledge. When I was an assistant professor at Ohio State, senior faculty members routinely visited classes and offered a commentary on the quality of the teaching and learning environment, with those comments later factoring into the junior faculty member's evaluation for tenure. I was working at home one morning. My afternoon seminar was to begin at three o'clock. The phone rang around eleven o'clock. It was one of the senior faculty members telling me that he would like to visit that day's graduate class. Although I had done some preparatory reading over the weekend, I had cut my serious and focused preparation a bit tight, but I said, "Of course," and immediately started intensive preparation for that day's class. Five minutes later the phone rang again. It was my wife. We were trying to sell our house to buy a farm in the country, where we could keep our two horses. She told me that a prospective buyer would be visiting the house that day at five thirty. She would meet the realtor and the potential buyer at that time, but I would need to spend a few hours cleaning the house. Knowing who my real boss was, I dutifully spent the next hours not preparing for class but cleaning, and I came to class as unprepared as I had ever been in my life.

It was one of the best classes I ever taught. How could that be? Ironically, because I had so little to offer, I spent the entire three hours pulling things out of the students, asking them one question after another, leading them to see a very rich world in the two long and complex poems by Hölderlin that were the subject of the class. Granted, I could draw on some previous knowledge, but because I was not really prepared, I had to be one hundred percent attuned to what the students could bring to the class and the discussion. I also let them speak more than I usually did. I don't recommend this practice to assistant professors and have never consciously repeated anything similar, but I do recognize that sometimes the job of the faculty member is to attend more to the students than to the material. When we reviewed a contested course at Notre Dame that was supposed to be taught in discussion format, we surveyed both students and faculty on aspects of the course. When we asked, "Was the majority of class time devoted to discussion or to lecture?" the students said it was mainly lecture and the faculty members said it was mainly discussion. Cognitive intelligence does not necessarily preclude self-deception.

A student's capacity for oral articulation is further fostered by conversations outside of class with faculty members and other students. Students who engage the great questions seek out conversation to discover and weigh new perspectives as well as to put their own views to the test. Conversation is for students both a search for truth and an arena in which to practice and develop their capacities for argument and wit. Students who are liberally educated develop an instinct for asking interesting questions and for identifying important issues for reflection and discussion. By engaging such issues, listening to others, and learning to organize and articulate their ideas, they develop the skill of communicating clearly and persuasively. This intense dialogue, fostered by the asceticism of the intellectual life, nonetheless makes students more worldly and better equipped to engage others when they leave college.

My own decision to attend a small liberal arts college was driven by a desire to be in an environment where I could have many discussions that would allow me to develop a capacity for argument, a mastery of the spoken word, and a deeper understanding of the great questions. Although I grew up in a loving home and was encouraged to leave the local public schools, which I liked very much, in order to attend a very ambitious Jesuit high school, our conversations at home did not consistently engage the complex issues of the day. In retrospect, I do not think I was alone in having such an experience. We do not have a great culture of conversation in this country. Sports and entertainment are powerful forces, and they rarely provide an ideal context for cultivation of the great questions. Neil Postman has cogently articulated that we are in many ways "amusing ourselves to death." Our attention span has shortened over time, and ever more bits of insignificant information pass through our minds and our conversations. We are close to Aldous Huxley's vision that what is essential is being drowned in a sea of irrelevance.

I imagined at Williams conversations in small classes that would allow me to develop my capacities for insight and argument, and I imagined conversations outside of class that would allow me to explore great questions with friends. And what I dreamed, all became true. I can still recall my interview for a Fulbright Fellowship to Germany. It was a fair and demanding test of my ability to think on my feet, and though I did well enough to receive the fellowship, I knew that I needed to improve. A similar reflection followed the oral examination for my undergraduate honors thesis. As I continued to work on my oral skills, I looked forward to my one-hour oral examinations in philosophy and literature, which I had to pass for my master's degree in Germany. I thought it splendid that Princeton had a one-hour oral examination on twenty major works of German literature with the student and the entire department of ten or so faculty members, each of whom fired questions at the student. One of my fondest memories of graduate school is walking the campus with another graduate student as we peppered each other with questions, many of which led us to new insights on our own. It was both excellent preparation and intrinsically rewarding; indeed, it was fun, and we often interlaced humor with our most serious discussions.

During my years at Ohio State, I was very active in teaching and advising graduate students. I noticed that they often performed superbly in their written doctoral qualifying examinations, whether they submitted a research paper, a take-home examination, or an in-house examination. When they then moved on to a two-hour oral examination with five faculty examiners, including one faculty member from another department, they often struggled, at times embarrassingly so. I viewed this exercise as a prelude to a job interview and to the greater need to be able to think on one's feet when leading a seminar class, and I knew that the students could only benefit from more experience prior to their qualifying examinations. Because of the large size of our graduate program and the restrictions of the quarter system, with short ten-week sessions, only the most advanced seminars required a research paper. Instead of asking for more informal papers or requiring written examinations for the lower-level graduate courses, as did my colleagues, I started offering students the choice of an oral examination. Many chose this path, knowing how much they needed to develop their oral skills. Few skills are more valuable than being able to speak clearly and effectively. One business leader has noted, "Regardless of profession, we spend most of our time representing ideas to coworkers, colleagues, and potential customers" (Franke 19). The liberal arts setting, with its many discussion classes and formal emphasis on oral skills, offers students ample opportunities to develop such skills.

A liberal arts education seeks to bring forward a capacity for logical and graceful expression. Such an education is dominated by writing and rewriting, in some cases short and concise essays and in other cases larger, more complex essays. Students learn not simply to avoid the basic mistakes one finds all too often in seemingly educated persons: stylistic awkwardness and lingering grammatical errors; lack of organization, with an unclear or overly simple thesis; undeveloped ideas; poorly constructed paragraphs; and little supporting detail. Liberal arts students learn to develop in their essays a clear, complex, and challenging thesis; an inviting introduction; a logical and coherent structure, with paragraphs that flow appropriately, one to the other; consideration of alternative perspectives and integration of appropriate evidence; well-chosen language; and a powerful conclusion. Ideally, students go further still, bringing forward an original and distinctive voice and writing essays that are unusually thoughtful and deep in their analysis; creative and far-reaching in their evidence; and elegant in their language. Such students learn to write not only clearly but also concisely and efficiently, and they learn how to move and persuade an audience. Research indicates that the humanities orientation of an institution correlates with self-reported growth in the ability to write well (Astin, *What Matters* 226–27, 349–50), and at least one study confirms that humanities majors make the greatest progress in writing (Bok 89). Not all graduates advance in this way; on average, engineering majors report that their writing did not improve in college (Astin, *What Matters* 228).

Most aspiring students can still remember when they learned this or that lesson in advanced stylistics. It is exciting to begin to develop a true mastery of a language. In a senior seminar at Williams on the philosopher Hegel's difficult and complex *Phenomenology of Spirit*, I noticed that students tended to underline the text in different ways. Some highlighted passages that they understood and found crucial to unlocking the larger arguments. Others put question marks in the margins beside passages they did not yet understand, so that they could return to them or ask questions about them in class. One of our classmates, with a spirit of imagination and a love of writing, decided to read the text with neither a yellow highlighter nor a pencil. Instead he took a black magic marker to the text and for at least one major stretch proceeded to edit all extraneous words, crossing them out, such that they were no longer readable. Several of us noticed this and arranged for the teacher to call on this student to read a few sentences we were puzzling over. The student read the Hegel text aloud as if it were written by Hemingway. It was for me a lesson from one student to another about how to write concisely and make every word count.

A Notre Dame liberal arts graduate and Harvard M.B.A. once told me that when his firm interviews job candidates, they give them an office, a computer, and a choice of five topics from which they must choose one, on which they are expected to develop an essay in ninety minutes. Liberal arts graduates, I was told, tend to excel in this exercise, which is viewed as an essential test of thinking and of organizational and communication skills. This employer is not alone. For eleven years running, communication skills—the ability to write and speak clearly—have topped the list in a major national survey of qualities and skills deemed most important in new job candidates (*Job Outlook* 23). As far back as 1982, in a survey of 113 officers of large American corporations, executives were asked to select five out of a list of thirty-two traits that were most important to higher levels of corporate success. Topping the list were verbal communication skills (R. Warren 12). A 1987 survey asked CEOs what learning areas were most important for undergraduate majors in business; tied for first were "oral and written communication skills" and "interpersonal skills," two areas that are more the province of a liberal arts education than a business education (Harper). Not surprisingly, the demand for communication skills only increases as employees ascend the corporate ladder (Bisconti and Kessler 12–14). In such settings, one must speak to people beyond one's area of specialization. And to lead others, one must be able to find the words to motivate them, an exercise that transcends technical competence. John C. Bogle, founder and former CEO of Vanguard Mutual Fund, notes that business leaders must be able to find the right words to communicate "the highest ideals, words that convey purpose and passion and vision" (166–67).

Given the importance of communication skills, many arts and sciences faculty members work extensively with students on the craft of rewriting, inviting or even requiring students to submit drafts of their papers. This intensive and indeed repetitive activity is essential to the development of their capacities. Unfortunately, the number of faculty members giving extensive writing assignments in advanced classes at American universities is uneven; many colleagues mistakenly think that the liberal arts can be reduced to general education requirements, which, however, provide hardly enough practice for students to excel in writing. Students should be encouraged to choose advanced courses that include extensive writing, and universities could do more to recognize those faculty members who do assign considerable writing and do provide extensive feedback. Some universities and colleges, such as the University of Chicago and Williams College, offer liberal arts students opportunities for tutorials, weekly encounters between a faculty member and one or two students, which help them develop their writing, improve their listening and speaking skills, and sharpen their capacities for argumentation.

The most meaningful writing exercise for college students usually occurs with the senior thesis. Developing a topic of their own choice, students advance in thinking, in writing and rewriting, and in research, organization, and discipline, which are necessary analogues to good writing. Although the topic of my own senior thesis, Hölderlin's concepts of finitude and infinitude and his critique of the Germans, interested me greatly, I needed to exert great discipline in finalizing the manuscript of well over one hundred pages by a strict deadline. While faculty may sometimes lament having to read so many essays for a given class, I have never heard a faculty member complain about reading a senior thesis. When students meet such a challenge, which is obligatory at only a few institutions, such as Princeton University and the College of Wooster, faculty members respond in kind; they read such works with care and delight.

Not only students but also faculty need to rewrite their manuscripts, sharpening their prose and clarifying their points. The need for even experienced writers to revise and rework their texts is one reason why the frequent writing assignments in a strong liberal arts curriculum help prepare good writers. John Locke has noted appropriately that "it is practice alone that brings the powers of the mind as well as those of the body to their perfection" (*Of the Conduct* 174). One never ceases learning to become a better writer. When I was a graduate student, I wrote a forty-five-page seminar paper on Hermann Broch's complex novel *The Spell*. My teacher suggested that I publish the essay, and indeed, it was soon thereafter accepted for publication in a premier series at Suhrkamp Verlag in Germany. There were two catches. First, I had to reduce the essay to fifteen pages. Second, the essay was to be published in German, and the original was in English. Although I had written many essays in German, including a master's thesis of well over one hundred pages, I always felt, when writing in German, that I was expressing only about 95 percent of what I wanted to say: most of what I wanted to say was clear, but there was something missing, something that eluded me and was just beyond my control. I decided that I would begin by cutting the essay to fifteen pages in English. I was taken aback that the essay became better as I omitted passage after passage and polished each line. Everything superfluous was eliminated; only the core arguments, the essentials, remained. I then sat down to translate the essay. Again, I was surprised. I had pored over the text again and again, editing it to the point of diminishing returns, where any further changes only brought me back to earlier versions. And yet, under the lens of translation, I realized that the text had again become transparent. I found further passages that were insufficiently clear or precise. The essay became better in German than it was in English. I was saying more in German than I had been able to say in English, the opposite of my previous experience. The exercise taught me that with the right patience and perspective, any text can be improved.

Over the course of one's education, various writing manuals are often recommended. Strunk and White's *The Elements of Style* offers a superb basic introduction to good writing that any first-year college student should have read. Bernstein's *The Careful Writer* and Follett's *Modern American Usage* are excellent for drawing attention to misused words and incorrect punctuation and for clarifying difficult questions, such as continual/continuous, different from/different than, fewer/less, fortuitous/fortunate, may/might, reoccur/recur, or take place/occur. When I was completing my first book, I wanted to ensure that it was as polished as it could possibly be. At that time, the Modern Language Association had just published *Line by Line* by Claire Cook, an excellent book that offers an advanced account of strategies for editing one's own writing: eliminating weak verbs, ponderous nouns, filler words, and strings of prepositional phrases; clarifying antecedents for all pronouns; reworking sentences to assure parallelism; and ensuring that the subtleties of word order and punctuation are correctly manifest. To most people, Cook's book might have seemed dry. Because I was focused on editing my own manuscript, it was for me absolutely fascinating. I studied every line and enthusiastically recommended the book to a senior professor at Ohio State, who was himself the editor of our discipline's leading academic journal. He, too, was finishing a book manuscript. He reacted much as I did. He took it with him on vacation to some southern destination and told me that he did almost nothing that week but read the book very, very carefully. He smiled in amazement at how much he enjoyed it and how useful it was to him, an already experienced and even eloquent writer. Writing well requires not only good ideas and creativity, but also knowledge, practice, and discipline. Liberal arts courses provide an essential foundation for one's later development as a writer.

A witticism attributed to Woodrow Wilson reinforces the idea that we improve our writing by editing and in most cases by reducing the length of our drafts. Wilson was asked to give a sixty-minute address one week hence. He responded that he didn't have enough time; such a speech would require at least two weeks of preparation. He was then asked if he could perhaps give just a thirty-minute talk. Wilson responded that such an address would require at least four weeks of preparation. When asked how long it would take him to prepare a two-hour address, he stated simply, "I'm ready right now."

———

Students who enjoy a liberal education develop critical thinking skills. Students learn to unearth and question their own assumptions as well as those of others. The common practices of one's own culture are subjected to a higher measure, namely, reason. Students quickly learn that this modus operandi is not simply an abstraction; it affects everything they do and choose to do. I can still recall a class during my first semester at college. Having spent more than a month on Plato's early and middle dialogues, we had just been given the assignment of writing a paper on the Socratic method. One of the students tentatively and cautiously raised her hand to ask how long the paper should be. To all of us students, this seemed like a very appropriate, perhaps even an obvious, question. The professor responded, with a smile in his voice, that it was the silliest question he had ever heard. The paper should be as long as it needs to be in order for the student to say what he or she has to say—neither shorter, nor longer. I was grateful for the lesson that what mattered were not conventions and expectations but arguments. What we had been reading in Plato had somehow come even more to life.

A liberal arts education encourages students to challenge ideas that may be widely shared but lack merit; in this sense, it shields against bias and fosters independence of thought, that is, a liberal mind. Students majoring in the arts and sciences become adept at recognizing and defining problems. They bring an array of heuristic categories to the phenomena before them and learn to make appropriate distinctions. A liberal arts education teaches them to review evidence carefully and thoroughly. They see through quick-and-easy answers. It helps them understand the consequences of a theory, a position, or an argument. Students learn to weigh sometimes contradictory and disparate evidence. They learn to recognize whether a reason is compelling or flawed. Studies have shown that students who take more courses in the arts and sciences experience greater gains in critical thinking skills and that the humanities orientation of an institution correlates with self-reported growth in the ability to think critically.[2]

Liberal arts students also develop the capacity to find solutions. Research indicates that the liberal arts foster "the development of higher-order problem-solving skills" (Pascarella and Terenzini 1: 147). The ability to identify, formulate, and solve complex problems is one of the most valuable skills sought by any enterprise. In developing this capacity, students draw on multiple methods. They acquire the ability to identify the most pertinent information for the solution of a problem. They learn to base their claims on observation, experimentation, and evidence. They learn to test and weigh hypotheses. They become familiar with quantitative methods in gathering and processing as well as in analyzing and interpreting data. They gain experience in thinking creatively and in conceptualizing issues in novel ways. They learn how to observe, make hypotheses, predict results, and organize and conduct experiments. They also recognize that value judgments cannot be answered by any number of facts alone and so know to address some problems through reflection on morals and values, for which their internalization of the principles of clear reasoning becomes essential.

———

Liberal arts students learn to focus, to attend to an issue; they gain the ability to think through a thought, to see its consequences and previously hidden ramifications, its connections to diverse spheres of knowledge. They learn to identify all of the relevant factors and to analyze them and their ripple effects. They develop a capacity to anticipate outcomes. Patience and persistence, discipline and diligence become part of the student's problem-solving arsenal. Students find the perseverance necessary for solving complex puzzles and the emotional strength to see an issue through to its conclusion, however unappealing that conclusion might be. Even in those courses that students may find challenging they gain a familiarity with difficult material that asks them to stretch their thinking and to develop the formal virtue of increasing their power of attention (Weil). This, too, is an experience and a skill on which graduates can draw. By availing themselves of the formal virtues that are developed in such contexts, students acquire a broader temporal horizon, recognizing that what is most useful and purposeful might in fact involve looking beyond the immediate realm and toward longer-term goals.

Each liberal arts student explores an engaging set of meaningful questions in some depth, which adds not only to the capacity for focus but also to the development of intellectual passion. Through immersion in the major or concentration, be it economics or physics or English, students discover and develop their intellectual passions and special capacities. In pursing the questions of their discipline, students become familiar with its methods, debates, and subquestions, and they cultivate an interest that gives them intellectual satisfaction. To know and develop one's desires and talents, to understand what intellectual questions animate one's soul and which questions one is most adept at exploring—in short, to develop self-knowledge—is to unleash a level of creativity and initiative, of enthusiasm and ambition that can transform who one might still become.

Breadth follows from the variety of subjects to which liberal arts students are exposed, giving them an array of resources to help them understand issues across the spectrum of human knowledge and activity. The variety of subjects helps foster the attitude that we can approach any problem in the historical or contemporary world with a range of appropriate questions, a curiosity that makes all events interesting, and wonderment at the ways in which issues relate to one another. Students develop the capacity to be receptive to new ideas, to gather a wide range of information, to research and read diverse kinds of materials, and to organize information and ideas into a coherent whole. Not surprisingly, one recent defense of the liberal arts took as its title the recurring injunction in E. M. Forster's *Howard's End*: "only connect" (Cronon). Many problems can be solved only by integrating the insights of multiple disciplines. The capacity to synthesize a broad array of ideas and data is essential for good decision making on almost any issue.

Our need for persons with breadth may be most acute when we are suffering economic troubles, even if that is a time when the liberal arts may be viewed as irrelevant. A former English and mathematics major at Williams College, Bethany McLean, was the first person to uncover the problems with Enron, writing an article in 2001 for *Fortune* magazine, "Is Enron Overpriced?" She looked beyond the numbers and asked how it all rhymed. Geoffrey Harpham has argued that one problem associated with the financial crisis of 2008 was that analysts looked only at computations and failed to think about the bigger picture. The frequent comments heard in this context—"It was all so obvious in retrospect" and "Our models failed to predict this"—suggest a failure to take into account more than simply facts and figures. One needs numbers, but one also needs a framework in which to give those numbers meaning and value. The capacity to ask the probing questions that elicit appropriate frameworks are more likely to originate in humanities courses or combinations of arts and sciences courses than in technical courses.

Some colleges, recognizing the value of integration across disciplines, have introduced innovative courses that address a great question simultaneously from the perspective of several fields. To offer an example from my own institution, all sophomores majoring in the College of Arts and Letters at Notre Dame must participate in the College Seminar, which I mentioned above. In addition to focusing on the development of students' oral skills, each College Seminar addresses a great question that students approach by engaging classical and contemporary works in the arts, humanities, and social sciences. In my version of the course, students explore the topic "Faith, Doubt, and Reason." They read works in philosophy and theology and literature, they attend theater performances, they discuss great films by directors such as Alfred Hitchcock and Woody Allen, they visit the campus art museum, and they read sociological studies of the beliefs of America's youth and analyses of politics and faith in America today. The range of questions that can be explored, all focusing on this nexus of themes, helps students develop the ability to think bigger thoughts and ask broader questions. They understand, in ways that some faculty members have forgotten, that the great questions cannot be parceled out to individual disciplines. To the extent that this is done, the questions become less ambitious. Indeed, one of the greatest challenges in liberal education today is to convince faculty members of the value of transcending their disciplines and to ensure that students have the right set of courses for their developing interests. Students tend to think in terms of problems, not disciplines, and cultivating that wider horizon can be advantageous.

Many strategies exist to aid integration. At Notre Dame, interdisciplinary minors, clusters of five courses, usually with a capstone element, allow students to combine interests in a variety of areas. These minors are popular with faculty members and students alike. During my tenure as dean we saw the creation of interdisciplinary minors in Catholic Social Tradition; Education, Schooling, and Society; Journalism, Ethics, and Democracy; Latino Studies; Liturgical Music Ministry; Philosophy in the Catholic Tradition; Poverty Studies; and Religion and Literature. Several already existing interdisciplinary minors, such as Gender Studies; the Hesburgh Program in Public Service; Medieval Studies; Peace Studies; and Science, Technology, and Values, also grew dramatically, and other minors, such as Philosophy and Literature; and Philosophy, Politics, and Economics, continued to offer meaningful programs of study to students, as did our various area studies minors, such as African Studies, Asian Studies, European Studies, Latin American Studies, and Middle Eastern Studies.

Another strategy to help students integrate disciplines involves the use of learning communities. Often designed for first-year students and team-taught, learning communities create a more integrated learning experience by combining subject areas, by bringing together faculty from different departments, and by fostering student engagement outside the classroom. In one form of learning community, a set of two or three courses, which are team-taught, are offered in the same semester and enroll the same group of students for each class. This form is particularly abundant at small liberal arts colleges. In a different form of learning community, two courses in separate departments meet in common at regular intervals during the semester. The opportunities for cross-pollination between the two courses are fostered by shared reading assignments and by a public speaker who addresses issues of mutual interest in a public lecture and in a special seminar for students of both courses. Courses can be conjoined in various ways: by sharing a historical period (such as the Renaissance), a geographical area (such as Latin America), or a topical focus (such as perspectives on the environment). Both forms of learning communities aid in the integration of disciplines and stimulate student-student conversation outside of class.

One important area of integration, not fully covered at most schools, is academic advising, the process by which a student and faculty member develop a set of courses that ensures a generating principle or pattern of meaning, where various courses complement and reinforce one another. Because this level of advising may not easily coordinate with the time demands on faculty members, students must be attentive to how their selection of courses mediates between offering them a breadth of skills and some kind of meaningful pattern. One idea, which I have not seen realized at any institution, would be a Web-based listing of courses with links to other courses, often in neighboring disciplines, which have similar thematic interests or develop complementary skills. Another way to foster such coherence would be to ask students to write each year a short essay for their advisor on how the learning experiences in their classes reinforce one another and how future classes can complement or expand those interests.

The value of understanding issues across a range of disciplines has only increased in importance, as advancements in knowledge mean that more and more issues are turned over to specialists and experts who may understand a piece of a puzzle but not its interconnection and integration with other, seemingly unrelated issues. In the world of work, as managers gain higher levels of authority, their responsibilities broaden, such that they must develop knowledge of new fields, learn how to acquire diverse kinds of information, and synthesize ideas and materials from areas with which they may have previously been unfamiliar. The liberal arts student knows how to connect disciplines and to ask penetrating questions across the range of human experience.

A liberal arts education involves breadth not only across the spectrum of the arts and sciences. It encompasses certain human capacities that are not in the least reducible to academic knowledge, even if they can be aided by study. Through the full range of their college experience, liberal arts students ideally develop capacities in all the multiple intellectual faculties that have been identified by Howard Gardner and other researchers. Gardner, who helped pioneer the concept of multiple intelligences, defines an "intelligence" as "the ability to solve problems, or to create products, that are valued within one or more cultural settings" (*Frames* x). Even if some capacities will be developed more fully than others, a liberal arts setting should seek to develop all of them to some degree:

> *bodily-kinesthetic intelligence:* the capacity to move one's body with some level of agility and sophistication in order to create objects or accomplish tasks;
>
> *spatial intelligence,* a sensibility for visual and spatial phenomena;
>
> *musical intelligence,* skill in the creation, performance, and/or appreciation of musical patterns;
>
> *logical-mathematical intelligence,* experience in analyzing problems logically, performing mathematical operations, and investigating issues scientifically;
>
> *naturalistic intelligence,* an ability to recognize and classify species of plants and animals and to recognize naturalistic patterns in one's environment;
>
> *linguistic intelligence,* the development of sophisticated capacities to create and interpret language, to learn one or more foreign languages, and to employ language to achieve goals;
>
> *intrapersonal intelligence,* or self-knowledge, an awareness of one's own needs, capacities, and interests;
>
> *interpersonal or social intelligence,* an ability to understand others, to make distinctions among them, and to relate to them in productive ways;
>
> *moral intelligence,* the capacity to discern good and evil, even in complex cases, and to act accordingly;
>
> and *existential intelligence,* a sensibility for the spiritual and existential, including an appreciation for ultimate questions and an interest in the infinite and ineffable.[3]

Liberal arts graduates take advantage of a well-rounded view of what it means to be human across time and place. They draw on their understanding of human relations, motivations, and activities, their sense and appreciation of human diversity and historical change, their encounters with diverse eras in time and different parts of the world, including social structures and political institutions, languages, stories, and cultural expressions as well as physical environments. They explore the histories, cultures, and identities of people not like themselves and develop thereby both a sympathetic and critical understanding of difference. Their recommendations and decisions reflect an awareness of this wider world and the ability to see an issue from a variety of viewpoints. This is important not only for individuals but for the United States as a nation. While the world admires American idealism, it has little patience for American triumphalism and American ignorance about the rest of the world. On the contrary, the collective image of the United States abroad, which is important for our efficacy, both culturally and politically, is greatly enhanced when Americans abroad are able to exhibit meaningful curiosity about other parts of the world, including what we can learn from the ways in which their customs differ from our own.

As students reach higher levels of linguistic competence, partly by spending time abroad, they learn not only words but also categories and concepts, finer nuances and broader ways of seeing, that may not be as prominent in their native languages or cultures (Schopenhauer). To learn a language well is to expand one's intellectual resources and horizon and one's sensibility for meaning. Students at liberal arts colleges are four times more likely to study a foreign language than other college students and four times more likely to study abroad (S. Lewis 127). In 2006, a liberal arts college, Goucher College, became the first American institution to require all its undergraduates to study abroad. Fortunately, even in fields beyond the liberal arts the percentage of students who study abroad is increasing (*Open Doors*). For many students, the time away becomes the most formative experience of their undergraduate education. They experience diversity and discover themselves, as they learn to navigate in a new and challenging environment.

Students studying abroad not only develop an enhanced curiosity about other cultures and a greater self-awareness, they also see the United States with fresh eyes, recognizing that what was often taken for granted is just one way of doing things. The immediate becomes filtered through reflection. Research shows that students living abroad acquire a critical distance to the conventions of their home country and develop, especially through a sustained experience abroad, a greater interest in international affairs and in problems that transcend their home country (Kauffmann et al. 74–83). Such students learn to become what Martha Nussbaum calls "citizens of the world."[4] An understanding of people, of culture, of place and a corresponding awareness of alternatives allows them to bring more than technical expertise to their professional challenges. These are useful characteristics, as virtually all spheres of life, not least of all business, are becoming more international at every turn.

With the openness and competition of globalization, which writers such as Thomas Friedman have sought to chronicle, students need to know more and become more comfortable in a wider world. Increasingly, firms recognize this, and they are becoming aware of the gap between what they need in an employee and what they are getting. A recent survey in which employers evaluated college graduates' preparedness in key areas revealed that "global knowledge" was rated the lowest of twelve different areas ("How Should" 3). Another employer survey identified competency in "foreign languages" as the most frequent deficiency among four-year college graduates (*To Read* 80)

In the fall of my sophomore year at Williams, I was struggling to read stories and novels by Rilke, Kafka, and Mann in the original German and having to look up too many words. I resolved one night that I would make my way to Germany as quickly as possible, so as to advance truly in the language, or I would focus on other subjects. I went to Bonn that spring. Those six months abroad and then a further two years in Tübingen were among the most pivotal of my entire development. Why? First, everything I saw was a learning experience—everything. It was all new to me, and I soaked up the language, developed an insatiable curiosity about German history, German literature, German philosophy, German politics. Because I was living in Germany, I had an existential connection to everything I was learning. As I noted above, research tells us that students learn more when they have an existential interest in the subject, when they are passionate about it or fascinated by it, one of several reasons why a senior thesis chosen by the student is such a valuable learning experience.

Second, I found tight communities of learning, where I was able to discuss issues with peers and engage them at deep levels. In Tübingen, the professors would have a beer or a hot chocolate with students after class, and discussions would continue in the pub or the coffee house. Because there was so little structure in the classes, with few, if any, clear assignments, learning derived from the students themselves, and our advancement had as much to do with us and our conversations as with what was going on in class. We had to take the initiative, but that was not a problem; the questions we raised with one another were great questions. Here, too, important learning principles were at play: that students be active in the learning process (instead of sitting back and listening to lectures), that students have a deeper connection to faculty members, and that students learn from one another. Such explorations had no bounds. I can even remember discussions with fellow students in the swimming pool: What were the differences in the ways that East and West Germany taught the Holocaust? Which of Shakespeare's tragedies was the greatest? How would contemporary science address Kant's cosmological antinomies?

Third, again and again I encountered challenges in my daily life that forced me to adapt, adjust, and eventually learn that this way of life was at least as interesting as what I knew at home. The time away from what was familiar gave me distance and led me to question much of what I had taken for granted. Being away from the local newspapers, with the occasional exception of a glance at the *International Herald Tribune,* turned me from a young man who assiduously studied the baseball box scores every morning to someone who didn't know who was playing in the World Series. I was attracted to other things, such as world political events, which had received so little attention at home. One clear manifestation of the way in which a student develops abroad arises when parents who can afford to travel to Europe arrive for a visit. This is one of the few instances (I grew up in the generation before five-year-olds made it a practice of telling adults how to work electronic gadgets) where there is a clear role reversal, where a son or daughter can navigate linguistically and culturally and show parents the sights and customs of the country.

A breadth of learning triggered by such experiences also deepens a student's capacity to relate to others, to interact and converse easily with a wide range of people, to understand what motivates and moves them. Interpersonal skills, which are valuable in any enterprise, are absolutely essential to effective business, both in the internal realm of management and in the external spheres of marketing, sales, and customer relations. Such skills derive not only from our early upbringing but also from our experience and our social and intellectual frames of reference. Students who master other languages, study other cultures, and live in non English-speaking countries or who explore issues relating to gender, class, ethnicity, and age develop an appreciation for diversity as well as an understanding of what makes diverse peoples both common and different, which helps students relate to people of varying backgrounds and engage them in meaningful ways. This range of experience gives students a perspective on issues that can illuminate societal problems, and it helps ensure a level of empathy that is a precondition for effective assistance to people who struggle for guidance or help.

Several institutions have found ways to create more opportunities for students to integrate their experiences abroad or to help faculty members model the diversity inherent in the liberal arts. Ideally, institutions offer targeted courses both before students leave for abroad and after they return, so that the experiences abroad are more fully integrated at home. At Notre Dame, where more than 50 percent of our students go abroad at some point during their studies, we introduced course development grants to motivate faculty members to offer more of such courses. The courses have been fun to teach, as the students' level of motivation and existential interest are universally high. Rollins College, a liberal arts institution in Florida, has introduced an innovative program to send faculty members abroad at least once every three years, so that they might better model global learning and think more personally about the global education of their students. "Going overseas has made them think differently about their classes back on their campuses and has opened up new areas of interest and fresh fields of study. It was, they often say, transformative" (Fischer). In order to promote faculty modeling of foreign language competency, Notre Dame recently offered funding for faculty members to advance their learning of foreign languages. Whether it would help them more in their teaching or their research, it would in any case enhance their roles as models for students.

━━━━

In addition to developing a sensibility for diversity, liberal arts students gain an eye for complexity and a tolerance for ambiguity, characteristics that make their perception of the world more animated and their engagement with the life of the mind richer. While some persons might believe that thinking one's way into complexities and ambiguities represents something muddled in comparison with the clarity of "practical" thinking, many issues simply are not reducible to an either-or dimension. Light is not simply a wave, nor simply a particle. To what extent behavior is influenced by genes or environment is not uncomplicated. Evil is not always revealed for what it is. Many great literary works are open to genuinely conflicting interpretations, which is a source of their continuing fascination. Some political decisions are tragic and represent a conflict between two goods: a leader with tragic consciousness does not simply choose the higher good and feel that she has made the correct choice; she senses also the loss of the lesser good, which is indeed still a good. I have been amazed at how often liberal arts graduates who have gone on to very successful business careers speak of the way in which business (and life) consist of gray areas of uncertainty, the unknown, where they spend most of their time and where they draw on the capacity to see an issue from multiple perspectives and to be comfortable making decisions that are ambiguous—and for that reason not necessarily popular.

Students learn to think issues through from every angle, and as new evidence is uncovered, they have the suppleness of mind to adjust their conclusions. In exploring the liberal arts, students see complexity where others see simplicity. They become more versed in the arguments for and against the important choices that face today's intellectuals and tomorrow's policy makers, giving them intellectual experience and confidence. By seeing all sides of an issue, they expand not only their intellect but also their capacity for understanding. An empirical study has identified intellectual flexibility as a quality that liberal arts students tend to develop in the course of their studies (Winter et al. 32–36, 65–67). Such an education also makes students more attuned to the diversity and intricacy of issues in the world. Students develop greater empathy both for those who disagree with them and for those who are less privileged. And yet, paradoxically, after surveying such details, they have a capacity to simplify, to see the big picture and recognize what is most essential in a given issue. Where others see only chaos, they see patterns and priorities.

A liberal arts education cultivates capacities that can be applied to all kinds of circumstances. Kant speaks of "the possession of a faculty which is sufficient for any and all purposes. It determines, then, no ends at all, but instead entrusts this to the later circumstances" (12: 706). Surveying a broader horizon and asking far-reaching questions are natural for liberal arts graduates. To borrow a distinction from the eminent historian Richard Hofstadter, we could say that liberal arts students develop not only intelligence, which Hofstadter defines as an excellence of mind that can be applied, in relatively narrow ways, to practical problems, but also intellect, which is more philosophical and is characterized by contemplation, criticism, creativity, and attention to further consequences, to being at home among complexities and within the framework of the bigger picture. Hofstadter writes, "Whereas intelligence seeks to grasp, manipulate, re-order, adjust, intellect examines, ponders, wonders, theorizes, criticizes, imagines. Intelligence will seize the immediate meaning in a situation and evaluate it. Intellect evaluates evaluations and looks for the meaning of situations as a whole" (25).

These ambitious skills and admirable capacities can emerge only when students are truly challenged to develop them, which means that faculty must hold students to the highest possible standards so that they can reach their full potential. Discriminating grades and detailed feedback are ways of pointing out strengths and weaknesses to students, challenging them to stretch, so that they are not lulled into thinking that they can already do what we want them to be able to do. Indeed, one of the character skills students should develop in an academically rigorous liberal arts setting is the ability to learn from criticism. Karl Jaspers notes perceptively, "Whoever evades criticism really doesn't want to know" (28). When coupled with ambitious learning goals and an explanation for the grade, tough grading is a gift to students that helps them understand that they aren't yet where they want to be. They can learn more. Students respond well to such feedback. Faculty who expect more of their students in a meaningful way tend to be more successful in helping them learn.[5]

I recall a letter from a former student, Kristen Drahos, reflecting back on her first oral examination,

> I remember walking into the Office of the Dean feeling nervous and intimidated. It was my first oral exam, and although I had studied and gone over the class texts numerous times alone and in the company of my fellow classmates, I still dreaded that my mind would go blank when asked a question. Leaving the room forty minutes later, I felt as though I was walking on air and that the world was mine to conquer. I had not only survived the exam, but I believed that I had done reasonably well. I thought on my feet, stayed fairly calm, and felt like I had used the material in an intelligent way. If this is learning, I mused, I never want to stop!

Ideally, liberal arts students are encouraged to stretch so that they desire to become more than they are and more than they thought they could become. Faculty need both to ennoble students with high aspirations and remind them that what they are now is not yet what they might become. Both of these principles—helping students perceive an ideal for themselves and drawing attention to their not yet having reached that ideal— are two profound elements of Socratic education and Socratic love.

———

A liberal arts education fosters, not least of all through its discussion format, a hunger for knowledge and an innate curiosity, a love of ideas and a passion for meaningful information, a fascination with new discoveries. Liberal arts students gain an interest in ideas and intellectual puzzles for their own sake, and as they develop new knowledge and skills, their palette of problem-solving skills expands, and their desire for even more strategies increases. A love of learning that encourages the capacity to continue to learn is the greatest hallmark of a liberal arts education. Liberal arts students understand how to adapt to a rapidly changing world, which gives them confidence as they tackle projects in new areas. True education, as opposed to mere training, includes, as Michael McPherson suggests, "the ability to respond to new situations and challenges" (14).

John Dewey notes that "the aim of education is to enable individuals to continue their education" (100). Education is not preparation for a career, but preparation for continual learning. Dewey adds, "To predetermine some future occupation for which education is to be a strict preparation is to injure the possibilities of present development and thereby to reduce the adequacy of preparation for a future right employment" (310). The capacity for change and innovation is especially important in an environment that requires dramatic shifts in employer and employee tasks and projects as technology, cultural contexts, and market forces change. A young American today with at least two years of college can expect to change jobs at least eleven times before retirement (Sennett 22). Not surprisingly, in a national survey, CEOs made clear that they "value the *long-term* outcomes of a college education—those that prepare one not only for a first job but for a long and variable career. . . . They insist that a college education produce people of strong character with generalized intellectual and social skills and a capacity for lifelong learning" (Hersh, "Liberal" 30–31).

Liberal arts graduates are more likely than more technically trained students to engage after college in the kinds of broad learning experiences that prepare them for unanticipated developments and new discoveries (Pascarella and Terenzini 1: 111). They are also more likely to take continuing education courses for intellectual growth and personal development (Pascarella, Wolniak et al. 80). In addition, arts and sciences majors are five times more likely than other majors to pursue a Ph.D. (Goyette and Mullen 524). Prepared to continue to learn, liberal arts graduates, whatever their path after college, develop a dexterity and vitality of mind and are eager to transfer their skills to new problems and positions. They can adapt as the world changes and as they themselves change. They bring a fresh perspective to problems and do not simply accept as given whatever previous practices may have been in vogue. They are constantly preparing themselves for jobs that have yet to be invented.

A traditional piece of advice for a young person is to major in business and go into a safe field, such as banking. The financial crisis of 2008 triggered an amusing cartoon in the *New Yorker*, in which an older person advises a younger person at a cocktail party, "A banker, eh? Can you make a living at that?" There is no predicting what kinds of positions graduates will need to seek in the coming years, but one thing is certain: they will require flexibility, dexterity, and a willingness to learn what is not yet on the horizon. Thomas Friedman writes about our rapidly changing, global world: "You want constantly to acquire new skills, knowledge, and expertise that enables you constantly to be able to create value. . . . Being adaptable in a flat world, knowing how to 'learn how to learn,' will be one of the most important assets any worker can have, because job churn will come faster, because innovation will happen faster" (239). Broad education, not technical training, makes one more likely to be inventive and to adjust easily to new innovations. David Kearns, former CEO of Xerox, notes that "the only education that prepares us for change is *liberal education*. In periods of change, narrow specialization condemns us to inflexibility— precisely what we do not need. We need the flexible intellectual tools to be problem solvers, to be able to continue learning over time" (vi). Not surprisingly, some North American business schools are integrating liberal arts courses into their M.B.A.

programs, recognizing the value of educating future managers who can "think more nimbly across multiple frameworks, cultures, and disciplines" (L. Wallace).

———

The various intellectual virtues outlined here are not only their own reward and integral to the life of the mind, they are also applicable in a very practical way. Whereas business graduates tend to earn more than do liberal arts graduates in the initial years after graduation, liberal arts graduates often overtake their business counterparts in the course of their careers. A range of studies document that in ever-higher levels of management, a greater proportion of managers hold liberal arts degrees. In outlining these studies, Michael Useem writes, "As liberal arts graduates climb the corporate ladder, they often become advantaged. The immediate employment gains of a practical course of study may come at the sacrifice of ultimate career gains."[6] Companies "rate a liberal arts education as particularly useful for performance in the top managerial ranks" (Useem, *Liberal Education* 115). As a result, the "hiring of liberal-arts graduates is often viewed as a long-term strategy for managerial development" (Useem, *Liberal Education* 38). A study of 625 employers of college graduates concluded, "As time in a career increases, broad liberal arts skills become more important than specific business-related skills" (R. Warren 4). A survey of nearly four hundred companies across a range of fields revealed that 85 percent of them hire English majors even when English majors lack training in the defining area of the corporation (Orange 7).

A longitudinal study of one corporation revealed that humanities and social science majors outperformed others, including business and engineering majors, in an array of areas, from creativity in solving business problems and range of interests to communication skills and interpersonal skills; these majors also advanced on average to higher levels of management within the corporation (Howard). Another interpretation of the same data set stressed the extent to which humanities and social science graduates excel in leadership skills and noted, "One overall conclusion from these data is that there is no need for liberal arts majors to lack confidence in approaching business careers. The humanities and social science majors in particular continue to make a strong showing in managerial skills and have experienced considerable business success" (Beck 13). In emphasizing the difference between training and education, one executive states unequivocally that a liberal arts education "is the optimal vehicle in undergraduate years for preparing for a business management career" (Benoliel 118).

Not all of the recent research suggests that liberal arts graduates outperform others. In some cases, the data suggest that those students whose majors focus on quantitative skills excel, including not only those who major in economics, mathematics, or physics but also those who major outside of the liberal arts, in fields such as accounting, computer science, and engineering (Pascarella and Terenzini 2: 496–97, 503–9, 540–41). Much depends on the quality of the institution where one received one's liberal arts education and the cultural norms of the firms in question. Graduates of highly selective liberal arts institutions, many of whom pursue an advanced degree at major research universities, tend to do very well independently of major.[7] Also, the values and preferences of individuals matter. One study, for example, suggests that humanities majors "are especially interested in having creative jobs that allow for independence, even at the cost of lower income" (Katchadourian and Boli 86). In the long run and on average, liberal arts graduates who pursue a career in business can expect to compete with business and engineering majors, especially at the highest levels of corporate leadership, despite having less technical knowledge of the fields in question as they start their careers.

How is it that liberal arts graduates flourish in business? Because they have developed the basic skills that are requisite for success in any enterprise: how to recognize what is of greater and lesser value, how to analyze complex problems, how to research analogous situations, how to formulate clear and stimulating questions, how to listen carefully and attentively, how to imagine alternative solutions, how to recognize patterns and reflect on counter-examples, how to sort through conflicting claims, how to prepare a cogent argument, and how to express it eloquently. In a liberal arts environment, one learns how to think on one's feet and how to think outside the box. What liberal arts students may lack in nuts-and-bolts knowledge of business, they compensate for with their abilities to draw on a breadth of general knowledge, to think creatively and communicate effectively, to adjust to evolving or unexpected circumstances, and to generate and evaluate new ideas. A recent collaborative study has argued that a liberal education is not something that should be restricted to liberal arts institutions or liberal arts majors but is in the twenty-first century "a necessity for all students," including students who major in applied and vocational disciplines (*College Learning* 20).

Vocational training is often limited and impractical in comparison with learning how to communicate clearly, think critically, understand others, and integrate spheres of knowledge. The acquisition of these capacities is a better long-term investment for work and life than courses in, say, fashion merchandising, human resource management, or strategic decision making. There are good reasons why the business world has sought out a writer such as Daniel Goleman, with his focus on emotional and social intelligence. The broad capacities Goleman addresses are central to the environment in which business majors wish to succeed. These human capacities, to which I turn more fully below, are no less essential for success than are critical thinking skills. Precisely because the capacity to challenge received wisdom is not welcomed in every hierarchy, including some businesses, students also need to develop capacities for empathy and diplomacy, which ideally arise through experience and feedback in superior discussion classes.

Even students with targeted career goals can benefit from a liberal arts education. The best preparation for becoming a premier journalist, for example, is not to obtain a journalism major but to major in an arts and sciences discipline and pursue an internship in journalism. The journalism major lacks the breadth of the liberal arts student, and so may not excel in the reading, writing, critical thinking, breadth, and boldness of vision expected of a strong journalist, but an English major without any related experience whatsoever is at a modest disadvantage as well. One creative strategy is to offer students, in addition to a liberal arts major, a small cluster of courses that help them gain familiarity with a more applied area. At Notre Dame, aspiring journalists major in any discipline of the arts and sciences but take a cluster of five courses, some broader in scope, such as the ethics of journalism, the history of journalism, or the media and the presidency, and some more practical in nature, such as the craft of journalism, taught by veteran journalists. Together with a summer internship, this program adds up to the interdisciplinary minor in Journalism, Ethics, and Democracy.

Surveys of employers regularly indicate that the most desirable qualities of job candidates are not technical skills. Instead, they involve liberal arts skills. In one study, 90 percent of CEOs queried called the humanities essential to developing critical thinking, and 77 percent found the humanities critical to problem-solving skills ("Wanted"). Not surprisingly, the leading businesses in New York City regularly recruit their management trainees from highly selective liberal arts colleges and offer them accelerated training in basic accounting and finance. Although Harvard University does not have an undergraduate business major or offer undergraduate business courses, a 2008 survey in the *Harvard Crimson* reported that "two out of five Harvard seniors entering the workforce" will accept "jobs in business, consulting, and finance after graduation" (Guren and Sherman). Directly out of college, liberal arts graduates also compete successfully for positions in, for example, marketing, public relations, and sales.

In the employer survey in the most recent *Job Outlook*, sponsored by the National Association of Colleges and Employers, the highest rated technical skill was "computer skills," which ranked ninth behind a combination of liberal arts skills and personal qualities in the following order of importance: "communication skills," "strong work ethic," "initiative," "interpersonal skills (relates well to others)," "problem-solving skills," "teamwork skills (works well with others)," "analytical skills," and "flexibility/adaptability" (23). While the personal qualities elevated by employers can be developed in any number of settings, the holistic orientation of a liberal arts education consciously seeks to foster them. Similarly, a study of more than 150 employers in the state of Indiana identified as the top three characteristics of potential employees: interpersonal communication, defining and solving problems, and teamwork; the highest ranking technical skill, computer skills, came in eighth (*Executive Summary* 2). It is not surprising, then, that some firms have introduced innovative educational programs for their employees that seek to foster, in discussion groups with scholars, broad capacities of communication and analysis, cooperation and collaboration, that are best developed through collective engagement with great works in the humanities (Franke).

———

A liberal arts education helps students make a transition to the worlds of business, medicine, law, education, public service, and other pursuits. Instead of taking technical courses, acquiring material that could be mastered on the job or in graduate classes, liberal arts students take courses whose content will not quickly become obsolete. While businesses can train employees in evolving business strategies, technical skills, and the firm's local culture, they are not equipped to educate employees toward the intellectual and social capacities that are best developed through a well-rounded liberal arts education. We often assume that we need to elevate the practical because of the necessities of life, be it to ensure that we ourselves prosper or that those in dire circumstances overcome their challenges. As a result, students in developing countries, not unlike first-generation college students in the United States, often focus their studies on business and technology, but what might be most needed to help developing countries flourish are broad and versatile problem-solving skills, cultural awareness, values, and leadership, which are better cultivated in a form of education that is not oriented toward short-term goals.[8] Societies must of course have a certain number of persons with specific technical skills, and students should always be encouraged to follow their interests and develop their natural capacities, but technical skills alone will not solve our most complex problems.

Also, within the United States, many seemingly strategic and practical problems require a wider horizon and greater cultural awareness. This is even more so the case today when American culture so dominates the world stage. A knowledge of history is important not only for business but also for politics. Consider the mistakes made in the wake of the 2003 U.S. invasion of Iraq, including a lack of wisdom concerning how to deal with the Iraqi people. Only four years later was a manual, prepared during World War II, re-released that offers advice for American servicemen and servicewomen in Iraq, including some basic background on Muslim customs and manners (United States Army). Wars are fought not simply through technology and power but also through ideas and relations. Moreover, we live in such a global and interconnected world that we need to be sensitive to the cultural contexts in which we operate; all of this requires a broad perspective.

My own experience as dean was not unlike that of a businessperson or politician who must draw on an array of capacities. First, articulating the vision of a college is a dean's most important responsibility. One must seek to motivate faculty, students, and supporters, and one must articulate, as clearly and as persuasively as one can, the distinctive vision and inspiring goals of the institution. While a vision can resonate in new ways, if it is to be received, it must attend to the inherited culture of the institution, which means that one must also know how to listen. Second, one must constantly assess quality, seeking to foster distinction and making decisions about resources, a process that requires a combination of establishing goals, gathering information and data of all kinds, and working through various budgetary options, so that one can decide how best to meet those goals. It also requires no less the courage to follow through on decisions that one believes are right independently of the political costs. Third, most of one's time is involved in solving problems, regarding issues of strategy or conflict or resources, for which one is constantly drawing on an array of categories and capacities that are not predictably tied to any schoolbook lesson on management. Fourth and related, another significant portion of one's time is spent dealing with people—colleagues who need mentoring, advice, and support; graduates and friends who might be willing to contribute to the college; students or faculty who have expressed concerns about this or that policy— and seeking in an almost pastoral way to develop future leaders and foster community. Fifth, one must give one's full attention to processes, details, and accountability, recognizing the benefits of efficiency and the importance of trust as well as respecting the distinctive values of the institution, such as faculty governance. Finally, because one enters such a position with the knowledge only of one's own discipline, one must be willing and eager to learn the debates and assessment strategies of a diverse array of disciplines. One must be willing to continue to learn. While I have found an occasional book on management or administration useful for a particular puzzle or task, the greatest insights have come from spending time with classics in the arts and sciences disciplines, works by authors ranging from Plato, Shakespeare, and Schiller to Dickens, Fontane, and Weber, which continue to remind us of our highest priorities and help us expand our capacities for understanding and empathy.

Fortunately, within a liberal arts context the selection of a major does not imply the choice of a lifetime career. In his persuasive essay "Major Decisions," James Burtchaell suggests, "The good thing about education is that it matters hardly at all what subject you choose to study. You can be educated in any discipline, because there is no direct connection between an educational subject and a specific career" (26). Any liberal arts major offers students opportunities to develop skills that will allow them to adapt to a variety of career options. As a result, the choice of major should not be based on career goals or on skills desired; instead, students should choose the intellectual pursuit that most engages them, that makes them feel most alive. Studying what gives one joy and delight energizes and exercises the mind and sparks curiosity, cultivating a passion for learning that leads to fulfillment on its own and prepares students to sparkle in interviews, especially when they are asked about their formative learning experiences to date.

As dean, I gave a brief address each spring to the eight hundred or so Notre Dame first-year students who had declared an intent to major in the College of Arts and Letters. I mentioned in that context that when I was a high school senior and applying to Williams, the application materials suggested that the reference letter come from a teacher in the area of my intended major, so I asked my high school government teacher to write the letter. During the following half year, when it was time to choose classes, I completely changed my mind. I was drawn instead to a distinctive major called the History of Ideas, which would introduce me to the great works of the Western tradition and at the same time allow for focus in the final two years, during which time I would begin my intensive study of German intellectual history. As it turned out, I never took a single political science class at Williams. That lacuna did not prevent me from overseeing a political science department as dean and thereby immersing myself in the debates of the discipline or from publishing op-eds in the *New York Times* and the *Chicago Tribune* before and after the 2004 presidential election. College taught me how to learn and to think, and those skills turned out to be far more important than the content of any one class or the selection of my major.

I was quite uncertain about what I would do after college, and that uncertainty had its appeal, because the many options all sounded interesting. I knew that I wanted to do something different, to continue my learning in some way. I heard about an opportunity to teach English in Japan and thought that would be a splendid way to learn another language and experience another culture. As part of the application process, I had to submit an audiotape, on which I explained that since the Japanese had trouble pronouncing "r" and since I was from Boston and often dropped my "r," I would be a perfect match. I was also required to send a résumé. I remember typing it out and feeling a bit uneasy that it covered only the top one-third of the page. Those were the days of typewriters, not computers, so I walked over to the library and xeroxed it, so that it covered the middle third of the page. I realized it looked just about as minimal as the original and no less odd but sent it along nonetheless. I also wrote away for an application to the Ringling Brothers and Barnum and Bailey Clown College in Florida, thinking that I could build on abilities I had developed as a juggler. In addition, I applied for a Fulbright Fellowship to study in Germany. If none of these were to work out, I thought I might travel around the country and work in restaurants as a cook, getting to know the United States a bit more thoroughly. In a sense, I simply wanted to extend my learning and could imagine diverse settings for that learning.

Often graduate schools and firms are looking for something distinctive on student applications. Not surprisingly in this context, arts and humanities majors stand out among applicants to medical school. In one older study, the highest acceptance rates to medical school were garnered by majors in music, followed by biochemistry, philosophy, and history (K. Warren). The most recent disciplinary figures reveal that at least six humanities or social science majors—philosophy, history, economics, anthropology, English, and foreign languages and literatures—have higher rates of acceptance to medical school than any of the diverse majors within the biological sciences (*Medical School 2002–2003* 30). Although the Association of American Medical Colleges no longer publishes detailed statistics by major, the composite figures are clear: from 1992 to 2006 the "rate of acceptance was highest for humanities majors" (*Medical School 2008–2009* 30). Humanities and social science majors who apply to medical school, generally smaller in number, bring something different to the study of medicine, allowing them to stand out from the crowd and enhance the diversity of the student culture as well as approach the subject with a broader horizon. Andrew G. Wallace, at the time dean of Dartmouth Medical School, wrote that "a liberal education is the best foundation for sustaining the values of our profession and for cultivating the kind of doctors our country needs most" (253). An article in *Newsweek* noted that "among the 2006 applicants to medical school, humanities majors outscored biology majors in all categories" and added that "even as breakthroughs in science and advances in technology make the practice of medicine increasingly complex, medical educators are looking beyond biology and chemistry majors in the search for more well-rounded students who can be molded into caring and analytic doctors" (Kliff).

Likewise, the best preparation for a legal career is a broad-based liberal arts education, not a major in any kind of pre-law program. Supreme Court Justice Felix Frankfurter was once asked by a twelve-year-old junior high school student how he might best start preparing himself for a career in law. Frankfurter responded,

No one can be a truly competent lawyer unless he is a civilized man. If I were you, I would forget all about any technical preparation for the law. The best way to prepare for the law is to come to the study of the law as a well-read person. Thus alone can one acquire the capacity to use the English language on paper and in speech and with the habits of clear thinking which only a truly liberal education can give. No less important for a lawyer is the cultivation of the imaginative faculties by reading poetry, seeing great paintings . . . and listening to great music. Stock your mind with the deposit of much good reading, and widen and deepen your feelings by experiencing vicariously as much as possible the wonderful mysteries of the universe, and forget all about your future career. (103–4)

What stimulates the imagination and disciplines the intellect, what brings joy in learning, is also the best preparation for a career.

For inspiration, Frankfurter did not need to look further than Oliver Wendell Holmes, Jr., one of the most powerful voices and greatest writers in American legal history. Holmes was an avid reader, freely discussing in correspondence his reading—from Plato, Aristotle, and Tacitus to Goethe, Tolstoy, and Melville. For Holmes, the law was related to all other pursuits: "If your subject is law, the roads are plain to anthropology, the science of man, to political economy, the theory of legislation, ethics, and thus by several paths to your final view of life. . . . To be a master of any branch of knowledge, you must master those which lie next to it; and thus to know anything you must know all" (219). Such knowledge is not unrelated to who we are and the lives we lead: "more complex and intense intellectual efforts mean a richer and fuller life" (79).

Students do not want to find themselves in the unenviable position one all too often hears older alumni lament: I wish I had majored in this or that liberal arts discipline, which really stimulated my imagination and continues to fascinate me, instead of this or that professional discipline, which I thought would be useful for my career. The college years represent a unique period in life, and a choice of major for the wrong reasons cannot easily be undone; indeed, at some level it is irrecoverable. Liberal arts majors tend to look back very fondly on their experiences: in a national study of some 11,000 liberal arts graduates, 78 percent recommended that students pursue a liberal arts education, and 82 percent stated that if they were able to revisit their decision, they would again choose a liberal arts major (Calvert 46–47). When graduates were asked what disciplines they wish they had pursued more fully, business did not make the top ten; instead one finds, in descending order, philosophy, history, economics, speech, political science, art or art history, English, mathematics, foreign languages and literatures, and psychology (Calvert 48,). Fifteen years after graduation, 92 percent of liberal arts alumni stated that they were satisfied with their careers (Calvert 125).

It is also remarkable how often one hears in conversation with alumni who majored in professional fields that the courses they most remember are the liberal arts courses in which they engaged the great questions. One such graduate of Notre Dame, who felt that leadership was crucial to every successful business, made a gift to support the study of leadership, not in business, but as developed through students' encounters with historical figures such as Augustus Caesar, Empress Theodora, Frederick the Great, Abraham Lincoln, Mahatma Gandhi, Winston Churchill, and Martin Luther King, Jr. as well as through literary figures and via perspectives on leadership in philosophy, theology, and the social sciences. Liberal arts graduates often continue exploring the life of the mind, recognizing connections between the world of ideas and the world of work. Shelly Lazarus, a liberal arts graduate and CEO of Ogilvy & Mathe Worldwide, said in a *New York Times* article, "As head of a global company, everything attracts me as a reader, books about different cultures, countries, problems. I read for pleasure and to find other perspectives on how to think or solve a problem" (Rubin).

Because liberal arts students constantly work with texts, whatever their major, they also learn the principles of hermeneutics, the art of reading and interpreting with imagination and precision. The complex or subtle work that requires careful reading and interpretation challenges a student's spontaneity, imagination, and intelligence. After students have contributed a few meaningful comments on a literary work, it does not take an overly discerning eye to develop those insights into an overarching interpretation. I try, mainly with questions, to bring the students to the point where a particular interpretation has begun to emerge. I then formulate the reading or ask one of the students to do so, and then I usually identify it with one of the students who contributed a major piece of that interpretation. As a group, we next look for evidence in support of the reading, all the while considering the types of evidence employed and the limitations that are to be placed on different kinds of evidence. As our interpretation becomes bolstered and our search for support continues, we ask many questions of the work and of the relative validity of different types of evidence, and we begin to recognize different and sometimes even competing readings.

We then seek to undermine our own primary reading by looking for blind spots in our interpretation, evidence that we have not yet integrated or were unable to incorporate. We return to the work again and again, seeking new evidence or raising unanswered questions. Whether or not we arrive at a coherent and comprehensive reading is not as significant as the fact that the students develop the skills both to ask appropriate and stimulating questions of a text and to weigh evidence for and against various interpretations. After each such inquiry, the students are thoroughly versed in the intricacies of a particular work. They are not seeking a ready-made solution as much as using their imagination and entering into active dialogue with the work.

Students who argue for or against a particular interpretation learn how to weigh and marshal evidence. The process develops both their aesthetic sensibility and their argumentative capacities.

It also cultivates an awareness of the need to be ever open to new perspectives and arguments. Ideally, students look for counter-evidence to the very reading they have developed. Attention to contrasting moments is a privileged dimension of interpretation. When the students write papers, they know not to ignore counter-evidence. They integrate the evidence proleptically, that is, they anticipate possible objections to their positions in order to refute those objections in advance. Simplistic readings, inattentive to the work's many layers, or one-sided readings, neglectful of those moments not easily assimilated, are insufficient. Complex interpretations that attend to conflicting evidence result in an honest relationship to the work and have the side benefit of helping students guard against dogmatism.

By teaching students the content and form of artworks, by confronting them with great and different traditions, but also by teaching them the mode of thinking associated with this process, we refine their abilities to analyze problems in the world as well. Because students must receive complex works with greater care and effort than much of what otherwise occupies their consciousness, the reception of such works sharpens their cognitive capacities. They learn a sensibility or sensitivity to subtle differences. At the same time, the cultivated experience of art and literature teaches them to look at the whole and not just at parts, to synthesize the parts into a whole. It allows them to recognize that meaning may unfold slowly and that the whole may be disclosed to them only as they recollect diverse parts and begin to discern patterns. It encourages students to weigh the significance of an event or occurrence or encounter and to imagine alternatives. It teaches them how to synthesize evidence, articulate a complex view, and draw appropriate conclusions. It prepares them to respond to life with emotion and sympathy as well as analysis and judgment, and it educates them to the importance of reason and evidence in an emotionally charged arena. To understand ever new facets of a great work contributes to flexibility of mind and an awareness of the need for breadth and balance.

This experience is not only its own reward; it is transferable to one's dealings with other works, other cultures, and the new and emerging challenges that face humanity. The intellectual virtues cultivated in a liberal arts context do not simply encourage individual success; ideally, they make the liberal arts graduate better prepared for life as a citizen of the collective, on whose judgments and actions the flourishing of a society or a state may depend. Among the most important principles of a democracy are a caring attitude toward others, including a willingness to participate in collective flourishing, and a capacity to seek common purpose and negotiate difficult disagreements through reasoned discourse; these are all central to the liberal arts. Insofar as a liberal arts education fosters formal virtues that serve both the individual and the collective, we can speak not of a strict opposition between learning and practice but of a "practical liberal education" (*Greater Expectations* 26).

———

In some cases, the challenge is not helping liberal arts students develop excellent formal skills but ensuring that they have opportunities to apply what they have learned. Some businesses do not hire liberal arts graduates; they think instead that they need business majors. As I noted above, some of the same firms that say they most desire communication skills hire business graduates and then lament that their new employees lack those very skills. To help solve this problem, educators and career centers could do a better job of educating businesses about the capacities of liberal arts graduates, a task that today comes with additional challenges. The economy has never been more competitive, and for a firm to educate its own employees requires an investment in human capital and invariably results in lost work time. In addition, businesses recognize that workers today are more mobile than ever; if they invest in educating their employees, they may well lose them. Those are genuine challenges. However, even as businesses anticipate a certain level of attrition, they need to think about the future. The most successful businesses recognize the value of identifying, recruiting, mentoring, and retaining employees who can make a difference for the long term. When I speak with successful businesspersons and ask them about their greatest challenges, ensuring future leaders is one of the most common topics, along with globalization and the effects of new technologies. My experience is not isolated. A 2004 McKinsey Consulting study of more than seven thousand global business executives reported that their "single most pressing business concern," after the "overall economic climate," was "hiring and retaining talent" ("McKinsey").

In this context, colleges might be encouraged to cultivate allegiances with firms which recognize that if they can craft a corporate identity that resonates with students, their new employees may not leave so quickly. Thus, internship opportunities that lead to jobs and partnerships can be appealing, as has transpired between General Electric and Notre Dame, where General Electric recruits a large number of Notre Dame students each year and seeks to develop in them a loyalty to the firm that might rival their loyalty to the alma mater. Voluntary departures are driven less by compensation and prospects elsewhere than they are by disengagement with one's current firm and its values. This is not often recognized: whereas 89 percent of managers believe that employees leave for more money, 88 percent of employees say that they leave for reasons other than money (Branham 3). Identification with one's firm or institution comes from experiencing trust and confidence in the firm's leadership, vision, and values; feeling that one's contributions are advancing worthy goals and are being recognized; having one's expectations and hopes for oneself and the firm fulfilled;

receiving appropriate training, experiencing meaningful challenges, having opportunities to develop and advance, and obtaining regular feedback (Branham). In this sense, the risks associated with employee education may be less than at first glance. Indeed, the very investment in workforce training can help build the trust that makes retention more likely.

By becoming part of the alumni network of a given institution, graduates who are employed in one form or another know what skills fellow graduates of that institution have developed. The alumni network is strengthened at colleges and universities where every graduate has had certain similar intellectual experiences. This network of associations, which in many cases crisscrosses the nation and the world, provides another element of utility to a liberal arts education. College is a locus for the creation of social capital and community, both among classmates and, after graduation, across the generations. The track record of success obtained by liberal arts graduates suggests that, although the highest purpose of college is the pursuit of knowledge for its own sake, colleges are accomplished in preparing students for the work-a-day world to which they turn upon graduation. In order to make this transition from the intrinsic value of a liberal arts education to social integration and a meaningful job, students must of course work to take advantage of the various opportunities offered by their institution's career center, such as engaging in a summer internship, attending a career fair, having one's cover letter and résumé reviewed, participating in workshops on interviewing techniques, and undergoing videotaped mock interviews.[9]

———

The idea that the highest end of a liberal arts education is learning for its own sake does not mean that this is the best strategy to defend the value of the liberal arts. On the contrary, in an age that is increasingly focused on competitiveness, credentialism, and getting ahead in the work-a-day world, the most effective defense of a liberal arts education surely emphasizes its practical value. Fortunately, the record is clear. In pursuing the liberal arts, students develop capacities that allow them to excel in any endeavor. The best firms know of these capacities, and they value them, especially among those employees whom they hope to see ascend into higher levels of management. To develop advanced skills in reading, writing, and speaking; to be able to think critically and solve problems; to have experienced a range of disciplines and spheres of knowing; to become comfortable with difference, ambiguity, and complexity; and to desire to continue to learn—all of these qualities prepare liberal arts graduates for positions and challenges that are available to them as they graduate and for those that have yet to be invented or discovered.

3

Forming Character

When the value of a liberal arts education is defended today, educators normally elevate not its intrinsic value, which is simply too foreign to contemporary culture, but critical thinking, which is essential to success and crucial to the venerable enlightenment goal of dismantling false truths. In the most recent survey of the Higher Education Research Institute (HERI), 99.6 percent of faculty identified developing the "ability to think critically" as "very important" or "essential" in college education (DeAngelo et al. 125). The other regularly recurring national survey, the Faculty Survey of Student Engagement (FSSE), asks faculty to assess the importance of fourteen different goals for student learning and development; "thinking critically and analytically" consistently ranks the highest.[1] In stressing the value of critical thinking, Richard Levin writes, "The essence of a liberal education is to develop the freedom to think critically and independently, to cultivate one's mind to its fullest potential, to liberate oneself from prejudice, superstition, and dogma" (15). Lawrence Summers stated in his inaugural address as president of Harvard University, "The university is open to all ideas, but it is committed to the skepticism that is the hallmark of education." Already in 1929, Robert M. Hutchins noted that one of the primary purposes of higher education "is to unsettle the minds of young men" (119). Faculty like to debunk the ideas of others, including students, and an old and esteemed tradition suggests that the first step to knowledge is knowing what one does not know. Not surprisingly, the second argument I have developed—with an emphasis on the virtue of critical thinking—arises in most defenses of the liberal arts.

The emphasis educators place on critical thinking, on liberating the mind from parochialism, is indeed important, but it is not exhaustive. Often neglected within a culture that elevates critical thinking is formation, the goal of helping students develop virtues, build character, and gain a sense of vocation, the moral and social purpose of education. Andrew Delbanco, a perceptive critic of higher education, notes that faculty are interested in introducing students to the academic disciplines and helping them prepare for well-paying jobs, but laments, "Any larger sense of purpose seems absent and there are few signs that anyone is concerned about it." The contemporary hesitancy to engage personal development and moral formation derives from many factors, including the strong "epistemological skepticism" that holds sway among rival versions of liberal education (Kimball 228). The elevation of critical thinking, with its implicit suggestion that liberal education means viewing everything with a distant and disinterested eye, seems to work against the idea that what one is studying could have meaning for one's development and identity as a person, for one's heart and soul.

For the ancient Greeks, education was not only about cognition but also about longing, motivation, and inspiration as well as attaining self-knowledge and developing virtues. In the United States today, the situation is different. Whereas the value of teaching critical thinking is universally recognized, a much more modest percentage of faculty identify "enhance students' self-understanding," "develop moral character," or "help students develop personal values" as "very important" or "essential." The figures as recently as 2004–5 were 60 percent, 59 percent, and 53 percent, respectively.[2] The FSSE report for 2009 reinforces these data: of faculty teaching at arts and sciences oriented undergraduate institutions, 93 percent place "quite a bit" or "very much" emphasis on "thinking critically and analytically," whereas only 50 percent place "quite a bit" or "very much" emphasis on helping students develop "a personal code of values and ethics." The figure for emphasis on students "understanding themselves" is similarly modest, at 57 percent.[3] It follows, then, that in the wake of partial faculty disengagement and students' elevation of practical goals, declining numbers of students report making progress in such areas as "personal development" and "awareness of different philosophies and cultures" (Kuh, "How" 105).

Our students' education is often reduced to mastery of information and the acquisition of techniques; it is rarely viewed as serving the loftier purpose of helping them develop a philosophy of life and preparing them to answer a moral obligation or discern a sense of vocation. But a college education is very much about articulating ideals, recognizing one's responsibilities to those ideals, and awakening a sense of wonder about future possibilities for oneself and the world. In short, it is about understanding, through the asking of great questions and the development of new capacities as well as through other formative experiences, such as conversations with faculty members and fellow students, what kind of person one is and what kind of person one wants to become. Late adolescence and early adulthood represent a privileged time in our lives for the exploration of new ideas and the formation of personal and social identity; as a result, for many students, the college years become crucial markers for who they are to become. During these years students develop, or fail to develop, capacities for integrity and courage, for diligence and self-sacrifice, for responsibility and service to others. They also develop, or fail to develop, a love of knowledge, a capacity to learn from criticism, and a sense of higher purpose.

——————

This idealistic dimension of liberal learning has not fully diminished in terms of student aspirations, despite some of the numbers cited above. Students have mixed goals, wanting both material gain and holistic development, both an economic return on their investment and the development of a sense of identity. The UCLA/HERI study *The Spiritual Life of College Students* gives strong support to the claim that students are looking for more than material gain: 76 percent of students report that they are searching for meaning and purpose in life, and 74 percent state that they discuss the meaning of life with friends (5), but in a related HERI pilot study of third-year undergraduate students, 56 percent indicate that their professors never provide opportunities to discuss the meaning and purpose of life (*Spirituality and the Professoriate* 1, 9). A recent national study of students and faculty in introductory religious studies and theology classes showed that whereas faculty consider critical thinking the highest goal, elevating it much more highly than do students, students prioritize the development of their moral and ethical values far more highly than do faculty (Walvoord 13–55).

As students complete their first year at college, the percentage who view "developing a meaningful philosophy of life" as "essential" or "very important" increases dramatically (Keup and Stolzenberg 35; Hurtado et al. 24). The trend continues into the senior year, where we see at that time also a significant decrease in the percentage of students who view "being very well off financially" as "essential" or "very important." Indeed, "whereas a significantly greater percentage of students were more interested in financial gain than a meaningful philosophy of life at the beginning of college, by the time of graduation the numbers had converged with regard to these two life objectives"

(Saenz and Barrera 14, 15). Similarly, a gain exists in the percentage of seniors, compared with first-year students, who find intrinsic value in a liberal arts education and in exposure to new ideas; studies show a corresponding drop in the proportion of seniors who view education primarily in terms of career and income potential (Pascarella and Terenzini 2: 282–84, 291–92).

The most common hope expressed by students when they embark on a new class is that it will somehow change them as persons (Light 47). Yet this idealistic dimension of education has diminished among many faculty members and even among administrators who are hesitant to address issues that take them beyond their specialized knowledge and raise complex questions of ultimate values.[4] Faculty are conflicted because many of them do want to have a substantial impact on students. Little has pleased me more than a student's comment that my course keeps her up at night (not because of the work but because she can't rest until she has thought more about the great questions we are pursuing or the artworks we are interpreting) or a letter in which a former student thanks me for having played a formative role in her learning, in pushing and encouraging her to develop her talents, or in pointing out possible options for postgraduate direction. The desire to have a broader impact on students is widespread, and so it is perhaps fair to say that faculty are conflicted as well, wanting to focus on disciplinary knowledge and critical thinking but also rejoicing when they have connected with a student in a deeper and more meaningful way. The seeds of such engagement arise not only in their teaching but also in their research, often in their very decision to pursue the vocation of faculty member.

Faculty regularly choose their topics for both scholarly and existential reasons. An economist decides to work on developing countries or the environment not simply because of the fascinating intellectual and technical puzzles but also because she wants to address problems facing humanity. An intellectual historian chooses to focus on Russia not only to engage intrinsically interesting works but also to try to grasp contemporary challenges in understanding the Russian soul. A political theorist works on just war to get a better sense of what policies should follow from the best arguments. My own dissertation was chosen for intellectual and existential reasons. I explored the concept of *Ruhe,* or stillness, which has a fascinating history in the German literary and intellectual tradition and has rich associations in religion, aesthetics, psychology, and politics. I chose to write a chapter on Hölderlin partly because of the fascinating narrative structures in his novel, *Hyperion,* but also because his work offered a magnificent and existentially significant account of a person's struggle with suffering. A chapter on one of Schiller's philosophical essays offered a fascinating set of conceptual puzzles but also allowed me to reflect on Schiller's efforts to combine the concepts of contentment and striving. Other chapters also had a combination of formal and existential attraction, and so it followed with other projects. A book on tragedy and comedy explored their fascinating structures but also asked to what extent tragic and comic structures illuminate the world beyond literature. Having taught German cinema for many years, I also became increasingly attracted to American cinema. What does a film such as John Ford's *The Man Who Shot Liberty Valance* tell us about the transition from an age of heroes to an age of democracy, and what is both gained and lost in that transition? How does Alfred Hitchcock interweave discontent with the present and the fascination of evil in *Shadow of a Doubt?* What complex images of America and of confession emerge from Clint Eastwood's *Gran Torino?* Such questions engage the mind and the soul, but somehow a number of faculty members lose the existential connection to their topics and so also their interest in helping students develop something more than simple mastery of disciplinary content.

The failure to help shape student lives during their formative years, to mentor them in values and ideals, is the primary lament of Harry Lewis in his *Excellence without a Soul.* William

Chace, who served as president of both Wesleyan and Emory universities, sounds a similarly elegiac note: "Those who arrive on most campuses do not now find what was once the mission of America's best colleges and universities: a commitment to the kind of moral development that produces an informed and responsible citizenry" (4). The idea predates the colleges of early America. For Socrates, learning was a path to self-knowledge and virtue. True to his emphasis on higher moral obligations and the world of the *ought*, Kant argued that one of the purposes of education is to prepare students not for the world as it is but for the world as it ought to be (12: 704). Empirical reality is not the last word but is instead subject to a higher standard. Education is preparation for an idea, a perfection that is not yet part of experience (12: 700–701). Not simply ensuring a livelihood, so that students can fit into the world as it is and make ends meet, education is for Kant one of the principal avenues by which a new vision for the future can be cultivated, one whose purpose exceeds the satisfaction of simply material needs and brings us closer to our highest capacities as human beings. The ultimate purpose of education is thereby to help make into reality the best that is possible for the world (12: 704). Ideal values form the standards for our action. Even if they are never fully realized in this world, they are a guiding principle and can be partially realized in our imperfect world.

Contemporary voices that are focused exclusively on the virtues of critical thinking or disciplinary knowledge speak against any integration of character formation as it has defined liberal education for centuries. Education to virtue, developing goodness and wisdom, is far more important for Montaigne than simply reading books and developing verbal dexterity. The good student, for example, learns to love truth even when it means uncovering positions contrary to those the student originally held; to be able to confess an error in the wake of greater insight, especially when that insight is one's own and not yet available to others, is "an act of justice and integrity" (174; bk. I, ch. 26). John Locke wrote: "'Tis *Vertue* then, direct *Vertue*, which is the hard and valuable part to be aimed at in Education" ("Some Thoughts" §70). For Locke, virtue is not unrelated to reason: "It seems plain to me, that the Principle of all Vertue and Excellency lies in a Power of denying our selves the Satisfaction of our own Desires, where Reason does not authorize them" ("Some Thoughts" §38). The German philosopher Hegel did not deviate from his time when he noted that "pedagogy is the art of making humans ethical" (7: 302). Benjamin Franklin articulated one of the founding principles of early American education, "The Idea of what is *true Merit*, should also be often presented to Youth, explain'd and impress'd on their Minds, as consisting in an *Inclination* join'd with an *Ability* to serve Mankind, one's Country, Friends and Family; which *Ability* is (with the Blessing of God) to be acquir'd or greatly encreas'd by *true Learning*; and should indeed be the great *Aim* and *End* of all Learning" (213–14).

In contrast, John Mearsheimer, in his address to the class of 2001 at the University of Chicago, "The Aims of Education," makes clear that today's universities do not, and should not, seek to help students develop moral sensibility, virtue, or idealism: "Today, elite universities operate on the belief that there is a clear separation between intellectual and moral purpose, and they pursue the former while largely ignoring the latter." To take another prominent example, Stanley Fish, at the time dean of the College of Liberal Arts and Sciences at the University of Illinois at Chicago, published several polemics against the idea that colleges should be involved in moral and civic education, culminating in his book *Save the World on Your Own Time.* Instead of helping students to develop a meaningful philosophy of life or helping them to discern their calling within a larger whole, according to Fish, faculty should restrict themselves to the teaching of critical thinking and to the content and methodology of a given discipline.

These skeptical and narrow views are sociologically predictable, resulting from academic professionalization and specialization, which recognize the faculty member's mastery of method and a discrete sphere of knowledge while insisting that integrative and ultimate questions be bracketed from the academy.[5] The view that moral development is or should be off limits also makes sense from the perspective of faculty members' unease with reductive versions of character development, which tend toward ready-made answers and moral and ideological indoctrination. The hesitation may be reinforced by a modesty about impinging on sensitive areas, which, it is believed, have as much to do with the private (and irrational) sphere of religion as with any other factor.[6] Further, much of what was once promulgated as virtuous was not virtuous at all; for example, behaviors and attitudes that were considered admirable in a society that failed to recognize the rights of women and minorities are now recognized as unethical. We can add that many who preach virtue are themselves not models of virtue. Molière's Tartuffe is only the extreme version of what we encounter regularly, whether in our personal relations, in public personalities, or in institutions. The fear of hypocrisy diminishes the voices of those who are modest enough to recognize their own weaknesses. But as understandable as this development may be, the separation of intellectual and moral exploration is ultimately irrational. As Mark Van Doren noted more than half a century ago, "The danger in separating character from intellect and asking it to operate alone is that men will then be licensed to handle moral ideas as though they were not ideas" (63).

This amoral vision of education is also hardly in the spirit of what parents expect. As much as parents express concerns about job prospects, they genuinely want their children to become good persons, and they expect that college will help their sons and daughters develop further, such that they become truly moral men and women. They may even hope that they will eventually become wise persons. A few years ago, Notre Dame sponsored a forum that focused on the university's distinctive identity. One of the questions we pursued was: "What do we expect our graduates to be like twenty years after graduation?"

The most that the skeptical educators cited above would be able to say in response to such a question is that their graduates will be smart people. Is that enough? Aren't they missing something essential? Religious universities may be freer about engaging issues of formation, but formation is not a question of religion. Regardless of an institution's affiliation, the overarching question is: are we developing only brains or also persons?

⸻

Character, leadership, and the cultivation of a sense of self are fostered not only outside the classroom. Although many faculty members would separate the inquiry model of the classroom from the formation model of residential life, the two are inextricably linked, and faculty can contribute to the cultivation of spirit and character as much as residential life can foster intellection. Many intellectual pursuits presuppose virtues of character, and so the two often develop in tandem (Schwehn). For example, to prepare well for each class by completing all assignments, rereading materials, making appropriate notes, and reflecting thoughtfully is to elevate study over other available pleasures and is as such an illustration of temperance. To renounce pleasure, despite its legitimate allure, for a higher value, is both a character virtue and an intellectual virtue. To consider that every author I study may have ideas that are worthy of my attention presupposes generosity of spirit. To recognize in the works we study insights of great value and a measure of greatness is to experience a level of modesty, which is not always common among the best educated.

Discussion classes test and develop many additional virtues. To listen carefully to the views of others and to weigh them honestly, giving them a full hearing with your utmost attention, even if they should contradict your own initial inclinations, is to practice a form of justice. To participate in the give-and-take of discussion by asking clarifying questions of other students, offering evidence to support your own positions, or proposing alternative perspectives in the light of disagreements is to exhibit respect for other people and for the common value of truth. To encourage effectively the participation of others and successfully draw good ideas out of them is to exhibit intellectual hospitality. To challenge the views of interlocutors without making the attack personal and thus without drawing their eyes away from the search for truth is to practice diplomacy. Humility is evident whenever I recognize that I must withdraw an idea from discussion in the face of decisive counter-arguments, that I haven't myself discovered the answer to a particular puzzle, and that I must continue to listen attentively to the views of others. To hold on to a view even against consensus when one is convinced of its validity is to experience social isolation for one's belief in truth and is an act of civil courage.

To search for truth is to be engaged in a variety of character virtues. The decision to pursue all evidence even if it should contradict or weaken one's initial claims is a mark of honesty and integrity. To think an issue through to the point where all angles have been explored and every ramification considered requires discipline and perseverance. A willingness to abandon previous beliefs in the light of more compelling evidence presupposes a capacity for flexibility and self-overcoming and can readily lead to gratitude to others for helping one along in one's intellectual and moral journey. Taking intellectual risks by exploring paths that have not yet been trodden and thereby sacrificing a much simpler and safer existence is, likewise, a form of civil courage. Patience and striving are both fostered when I recognize that, despite my best efforts to date, my tentative answers to a given puzzle remain inadequate, and I must continue to delve further.

To accept as valid an argument that has consequences for my lifestyle, for example, an ethical argument that might change what I do on a daily basis, is to undergo more than an intellectual transformation. To truly consider and, even more so, fully accept the validity of a position that is contrary to the values and identity that have formed me to date is to subject myself to a destabilizing break with the past, indeed an identity crisis, for the sake of truthfulness and consistency. Such positions presuppose self-sacrifice and courage.

Similarly, if we lack certain character virtues, then we will make intellectual mistakes. Arrogance leads us to think that our abilities are greater than they are and that we see more than we really do, which can lead to our dismissing arguments that might indeed be worthy of our attention. Similarly, if we become defensive or emotional, the clarity of thought needed to make a wise decision suddenly becomes cloudy. Cowardice, or the fear of criticism, can lead to an unwillingness to have one's own ideas tested (and improved). Not having the courage of one's convictions can mean that one is fully dependent on the (often aberrant) opinions of others. An indulgence in worldly things disproportionate to their actual worth can distract students from the focus and concentration necessary to handle difficult and compelling questions that require extended attention. Indifference ensures that the kind of effort required to explore great questions will not be present. Sloth and complacency mean that even if one has interest, one is not devoting the necessary effort and discipline to uncover what needs to be revealed in order to understand an issue fully. Envy may prevent us from recognizing the greatness in the contributions and ideas of others. Greed can lead us to elevate external recognition over ideas themselves and can even tempt us to dishonesty and the fabrication of data, a violation of one of the necessary conditions for truth and a culture of truth.

These insights are often overlooked, first, by those persons in administration and student affairs who do see college as involving the development of character but who hold the view that this development occurs solely though residential life and extracurricular activities, and, second, by those faculty members who view the classroom as a purely intellectual enterprise, devoid of issues of character. One reason why Plato wrote dialogues was to exhibit the ways in which ideas relate to various life-forms. Plato interweaves the criticism of ideas with the evaluation of persons. Individuals who are full of themselves, dogmatic and self-assured, are not likely to uncover truth. Interlocutors who are insufficiently self-confident to entertain views from the opposition will also fail to gain knowledge, so will those who have no serious interest in the genuine pursuit of truth. Someone, on the other hand, who is willing to admit his errors, to give up false claims to knowledge, is on the right path, and a person who is willing to risk his identity, reputation, and life in the search for truth is also likely to be on a meaningful, if potentially tragic, journey.

Socrates did not separate reason and morality but insisted that we must be able to give a rational account of our moral decisions, and not only give an account: philosophy for Socrates is about how we relate our lives to those ideas. This is clear not only from his discussions of piety and justice in the wake of his trial but also from his integration of performative contradictions: we cannot enter into the sphere of argumentation without presupposing certain ethical values—trying genuinely to understand the other person's position, seeking to make our own positions understandable, evaluating all positions fairly, elevating the principle of consistency, believing in the possibility of truth, and recognizing that ideas have consequences. It is not that one chooses to do so; these intellectual values and ethical virtues are necessary conditions of meaningful discourse, an insight that has been developed in our age particularly by the German philosophers Jürgen Habermas, Karl-Otto Apel, and Vittorio Hösle.

To engage in dialogue, to share an intellectual insight with another person is to experience a meaningful bond. Frontiers of knowledge are often advanced when faculty members and students exhibit teamwork and collaboration, working together on a project. Heinrich von Kleist has shown that ideas often emerge in the very act of conversation and dialogue. Complex problems require the insights of a wide range of disciplines and thus faculty and students schooled in these various disciplines. Learning and even scholarship are not simply technological processes; they presuppose a wide set of values and virtues that relate to character and a willingness to engage in the common pursuit of truth. Love, the highest of all virtues, is embodied in the most elevated form of learning, the love of wisdom, which is often attained in "trusting dialogue," that is, in a context of social and intellectual friendship (John Paul 46).

Except for religious colleges and universities, we may never return to an ideal of learning that gives no less weight to being good than to being smart, but perhaps we can find a more appropriate balance than has become the recent norm. Academic preparation and motivation are the two greatest indicators of success in college (Kuh, Kinzie et al. 7). For faculty members to ignore motivation as irrelevant or to overlook the wide array of character traits noted above is to lessen chances for student learning. Such abandonment may also reduce opportunities for postgraduate employment, given the interest among employers in integrity and motivation, in passion and discipline, and in interpersonal and teamwork skills.

———

One way to get students intellectually and existentially engaged is to have them work with one another. While faculty might be shy about exploring broader and more existential questions, students are not. Moreover, students learn tremendously from one another. Therefore, one of the best strategies one can pursue as a teacher is to help a class bond as a group and spend considerable time together outside of class, such that the intellectual conversation of the class is extended. In one of my sophomore classes, students had bonded so much that they had a reunion shortly before graduation. Another class piled into several cars after the end of the semester to see a play in Chicago that we had discussed in class. That same group of students requested another class together in their senior year. What strategies worked to get the students to bond as a group and spend considerable time together outside of class? Like most complicated problems, one needs multiple strategies. At the beginning of a semester, I have the students come to my office in groups of three or four for a practice oral examination. I ask them what kinds of questions they think would make sense. They usually come up with the appropriate genres: questions of interpretation and evaluation, questions relating form to content, questions of comparison and contrast. I then ask each student a sample question. I end by asking them what might be some of the best strategies to prepare for the examination. They usually come up with some sensible strategies, reviewing notes, rereading texts, anticipating relevant questions, and almost always someone will suggest, speaking with other students or asking each other questions or practicing together. If not, I mention this strategy, and in all cases I encourage them to work together in this way. Occasionally, in a final examination, a student will answer one of my questions by generously noting that a particular idea came from another student, which represents a wonderful blend of intellect and character.

The most important collaboration takes place as a result of students leading discussions in teams of two. I lead the discussion the first three or four weeks, to model strategies for them and to get the class on a particular trajectory. During that time they rank their preferences for topics, and I assign two students to lead each class, and each student undertakes this exercise twice during the semester. The group of two students develops up to ten study questions together, sends them to me, I edit them, adding some of my own, and then I send them out to all of the students a day or two in advance of each class. Each student must then answer one or two or three questions, depending on complexity, in advance of every class. Because students go through the exercise of preparing questions and leading class twice, they always work with two different partners.

Early in the semester I have the students come to my home for dinner, and I eat with smaller groups in the dining hall three or four times during the semester. In advance of our class visit to the campus art museum, students are required to go in groups of two to four to discuss selected paintings together, and then each writes a one-page description and interpretation in advance of our collective visit. Students in groups of two or three videotape themselves in discussion with one another, and then each one writes an analysis of the conversation, including issues of form; this exercise encourages greater self-awareness and helps motivate students to practice together in advance of the oral examinations.

Another strategy is to involve others beyond the class, to expand the classroom to other colleagues and students. We usually get together once as a group to meet with someone outside of class who might have interesting perspectives on our topic. The films we discuss are shown outside of class time, in the late afternoons or early evenings, and many of the students get together for a meal or discussion after the viewing. Those who cannot attend the collective showing borrow the DVD and watch it with one another in one of the residential halls. Students are also free to invite their friends to the evening film showings, such that one student reported that as soon as she arrived back to her dorm room the next day, her roommate pounced on her with questions about what had been said in class about the film we were discussing, Bolt's and Joffé's *The Mission*.

One assignment asked students to try to integrate the content of the course unobtrusively into their daily life. They were to tell Lessing's ring parable, a complex and beautiful parable, known to every well-educated German, about religious tolerance. I asked them to work the telling of the parable into everyday conversation, for example, a conversation about their course work or about faith questions at Notre Dame or about world politics and religious conflict. The first time I gave the assignment I decided I had better try it myself and wound the parable into conversation at a dinner with John Brademas, the former congressman and president emeritus of New York University, Rev. Theodore M. Hesburgh, C.S.C., president emeritus of Notre Dame, and several others. It was not difficult to find an appropriate opening, but it took some chutzpah to command the attention of two such powerful personalities and great storytellers for such a long parable. I could fully empathize with my students, but I could also see how useful the exercise could be for their development as interlocutors and storytellers. The students were to write a summary of their experience, outlining the context, how well they told the story, how it was received, how the discussion evolved afterward, and how they might tell the story differently the next time. They were also free to experiment more than once and report on their best adventure.

Another assignment was more direct. I asked them to conduct an oral interview with an older person about aspects of the person's faith journey. I reviewed each student's sample questions in advance but recommended that they be especially attentive to the possibility of follow-up questions based on what was interesting and fascinating in what they heard. We discussed the importance of setting and non-verbal gestures. The goal was to make it as much of a conversation as possible, to connect and to try to bring the interlocutors to the point where they were discovering in the course of the conversation things that they didn't know about themselves. One of the ideas behind such assignments is to break down the barrier between the classroom and whatever takes place outside, so that students become engaged with intellectual and existential questions on a regular basis. It also underscores the idea that the liberally educated person can speak meaningfully with anyone. Such persons "can hold a conversation with a high school dropout or a Nobel laureate, a child or a nursing-home resident, a factory worker, or a corporate president. Moreover, they participate in such conversations not because they like to talk about themselves but because they are genuinely interested in others" (Cronon 10).

Some of my most memorable experiences at Williams involved listening to my own teachers ask questions of guest speakers. It did not surprise me, therefore, to hear one of my students comment about a similar experience at Notre Dame. The department of history offers a one-credit course for undergraduates entitled Discovering History. History majors who enroll in the course attend lectures, films, and presentations for credit. One student told me how much she enjoyed listening to a candidate for a faculty position present her work. Not only the talk itself, which was interesting enough, but the experience of watching her professors on the other side of the podium, asking questions and relating the candidate's work to their own, gave her a perspective that helped break down the traditional sense of where and how learning takes place. Moreover, to see her professors excited about learning raised her own level of interest. Modeling need not take place only inside the classroom.

The first discussion class I ever taught was as a senior at Williams College. We were taking a seminar on Hegel, and each student had to lead one discussion. My class focused on Hegel's analysis of Sophocles' *Antigone,* in which Antigone refuses to obey the commands of the state and dies for her allegiance to her brother Polynices, to whom she gives a token burial in defiance of the state's decree that, for reasons of treason, he must lie unburied. In being one thing, loyal to her family, Antigone is not something else, loyal to the laws of her state. The chapter in which Hegel pursues his interpretation is complex and contains the seeds of his developed theory of tragedy. I opened the discussion with an overarching question, an existential question, if you will: "What does it mean to have character?" Students understood it both as a question of greater meaning and as an entry to our discussion of the chapter, including the tragic fate of choosing one good over another good. The students were animated, and the discussion was productive. I brought to class a set of questions as well as various ideas and strategies on which I could draw, depending on where the discussion went, even as I kept an eye on covering several main concepts in the chapter. That initial connection with other students helped to convince me of one of my life's goals: to engage in the exploration of great questions in dialogue with superb works and bright minds.

Since then, I have continued to find that undergraduate classes work best when, in addition to focusing on developing knowledge of the material and appropriate analytical skills, they also engage students as persons. In my College Seminar course Faith, Doubt, and Reason, students read a significant number of major works from a variety of disciplines, but in addition to reflecting on the works, including their aesthetic structures and intellectual arguments, students are invited to explore their own thinking on the topics, asking such questions as: What is faith? How does it relate to reason? Is doubt potentially productive? How do we judge the validity of a religious claim? How does doubt relate to identity crises and the development of a richer identity? What role does faith play in human relationships? Because the topic lends itself to existential concerns, students sometimes receive study questions in that direction. The majority of questions focus on understanding the texts, evaluating their assumptions and arguments, exploring their forms, and recognizing the works in their various contexts, but the questions can also address more existential interests. These normally fall into an optional category, that is, students, after answering one technical question, might choose a second technical question or an existential question, but the students are often drawn to a combination of the technical and the existential. For example, after reading Plato's *Euthyphro*, students were invited to explore whether it is still common today to ask a question such as, "What is piety?" and what factors contribute to the current situation. Students were asked if they saw anything of themselves in Woody Allen's *Zelig*. After reading William James on mysticism, they were asked whether they had ever had anything resembling a mystical experience, and, if so, which characteristics that James describes were involved. The answers might be far less important than the exercise of getting the students to think about the works as being of more than simply historical or rhetorical interest. Great texts can engage them as developing persons. Collectively as a faculty, we can probably do more to spark such deeper interests. Sadly, 43 percent of first-year students nationally and 27 percent of graduating seniors report that they "frequently felt bored in class" (Hurtardo 8; Saenz and Barrera 6). Whether these figures stem from a lack of student engagement or a failure on the part of faculty to organize their classes meaningfully and to inspire students is an open question, but faculty members do have the capacity to help increase student interest.

Particularly productive are invitations to students not to provide answers but to ask further questions. For example, my students are sometimes invited to write out questions about faith, doubt, or reason that interest them existentially or intellectually or both. These would be questions which, if answered, would help them in their own understanding as a person of faith or as a person who thinks deeply about religion and reason. After reading a sociological study of American religion and American spirituality, they were invited to ask what five empirical questions would they most like to have answered that were not already contained in the study they read and what use the answers to those questions might have for disciplines other than sociology. The request for questions combines two pedagogical principles—active learning and existential engagement—and fosters the habit of continuing to ask questions, which should be useful beyond any one class and beyond college itself. The fact that graduates of this class are now in law school at Stanford and Penn, are working for Google, are officers in the U.S. Navy, are teaching and doing research in other countries, are pursuing Ph.D.'s, and are involved in social justice activities says something about how a course with great questions can speak to different students in a variety of ways.

———

Clearly it is a challenge to find, develop, and reward faculty members such that the third and more ambitious goal of fostering character is met. Although graduate schools are better now than they were decades ago in preparing graduate students for teaching, there is still a modestly cavalier attitude toward this preparation, as if it were subordinate to research excellence. Graduate education rarely addresses the question of how to foster the development of more than cognitive abilities, and few graduate students are encouraged to address the great questions. If one leaves hiring decisions entirely to departments, then, depending on local culture, research alone could determine the hierarchy of finalist candidates.

There are several ways to try to address this concern. First, when a college holds interviews for faculty positions, the potential contribution of candidates to teaching and formation can become part of the interview process. For most of my tenure as dean at Notre Dame, I interviewed every finalist for jobs in the arts, humanities, and social sciences. With about forty searches per year and on average three finalists per search, that involved about 120 interviews per year over a few concentrated months, and over time close to 1,000 interviews. These interviews covered a candidate's scholarship, teaching, and potential fit for the University. Several questions helped me ascertain the prospective faculty member's love of teaching and potential contribution to our distinctive mission. Over time I looked for less conventional strategies, which tended to make the discussions both more interesting and more productive. Asking, "Who was your best teacher?" tended to get the very best candidates excited, as they talked about teachers who changed not only their thinking but also their lives. Even the affective response to the question told me a great deal. A large smile and the comment,

"What a great question!" was usually a prelude to a very animated and rich response. Another question I liked to ask was, "What attracts you about Notre Dame's distinctive identity?" This open question allows for an almost inexhaustible number of possible responses, but an inability to engage it in any meaningful way is a sobering sign. I also liked to ask, "How will your research help you as a teacher?" We wanted to hire scholars whose topics would be of potential interest to undergraduate as well as graduate students. That means scholarly topics that have been chosen because they are important, not simply because they had yet to be mined by others or because they are narrow and thus easily manageable.

Second, colleges and universities can become more strategic in orienting faculty members to their distinctive ethos. New faculty members are eager to learn about a college's customs and rituals, its history and vision, the residential life of students and other particulars. The first year on the faculty and the year after tenure offer wonderful opportunities for a college to articulate its vision and priorities and to cultivate solidarity with that higher purpose. Getting others voluntarily on board with common goals results in an intrinsic motivation, which is the most powerful form of motivation in any successful organization. It is especially important in a college or university, where conventional management styles and techniques do not apply. A dean is the conductor of an orchestra made up entirely of composers. One cannot order faculty to play the same music, but one can at times inspire them to play the same music or at least complementary music. The challenge is particularly difficult when the music is not the kind that they have practiced over the years. To adjust their habits requires a compelling vision that inspires them.

Third, meaningful incentives can help steer faculty members toward distinctive goals. I have always been concerned about the oral capacities of students and offered summer funding to faculty members who would develop new dialogue-intensive courses. That initiative brought several such courses into the curriculum. Likewise, we created incentives for courses that would be newly cast to integrate disciplinary topics with the Catholic mission of the institution and incentives for new courses that could contribute to diversity. One can create similar incentives for courses that include learning from peers or extensive feedback or multiple disciplines or an element of formation. In addition to employing one-time funds strategically, it is important that promotion-and-tenure decisions reward faculty members who excel in both scholarship and teaching, including teaching in the wider sense that I have articulated here instead of faculty members who are simply one-dimensional.

None of this is easy. Competition, ambition, and prevalent reward structures ensure that faculty members will in many cases devote as much time as they can to their research. Over the past decades professors have on average developed stronger loyalties to their academic disciplines than to their institutions, developing latent identities, in the formulation of Alvin Gouldner, more as "cosmopolitans" than as "locals." Peer review gives considerable autonomy to departments, who want to make independent judgments and whose loyalties within the institution are often more to their departments than to the common curriculum. There are exceptions, however, with some institutions fostering a combination of locals and cosmopolitans, and in ideal cases, faculty members who are simultaneously both—distinguished and dedicated specialists recognized for their research and at the same time colleagues willing to roll up their sleeves in advancing the local community of learning. With the effective cultivation of a distinct institutional mission, a vibrant sense of community, a narrative of local success, and appropriate reward structures, even further exceptions can be fostered.

To the extent that presidents, provosts, and deans can convince faculty of the intrinsic value of spending time with students, motivating them fully to embrace their calling as teachers, they should do so. To the extent that college reward structures signal values, colleges should recognize teaching as they do research, and not only classroom teaching. Prizes should be awarded for advising and informal mentoring as well as for classroom teaching. Colleges should make clear to departments that more is at play than disciplinary knowledge in assessing the potential contribution of a faculty member to a community of learning. Questions directed to job candidates that give one a sense of what animates them are no less important than ascertaining if they can publish in the top journals, and many universities, such as Notre Dame, will have a high bar that should expect excellence in both teaching and research and compromise on neither. I wrote well over three hundred renewal, tenure, and promotion letters as dean, assessing faculty performance for our university committee on promotion and tenure. I began every letter with teaching, so as to ensure that this value was not neglected, given the tendency, exacerbated by disciplinary focus and competitive aspirations, to elevate research. At the premier liberal arts colleges and universities, the highest salaries within a discipline should be not for the best researchers but for the faculty members who are the best at both research and teaching in the widest sense of the word. Those faculty members are often the ones who reach out to students for the simple reason that they love teaching and value the encounter with students for its own sake. Here, on the side of the faculty, the intrinsic and the idealistic overlap.

One way in which I sought to cultivate community at Notre Dame was to have a simple box lunch with a random group of seven or so faculty members about three times a week. I opened the meetings by saying that they served four purposes: I wanted the faculty members to get to know one another (the only sifting process was to try to ensure some disciplinary and gender diversity); I asked for their comments on how the College of Arts and Letters could improve; I invited their questions about anything within the College or the University; and I welcomed a discussion of whatever was on their minds. The full hour was devoted to whatever topics faculty members wished to discuss, and at least two-thirds of the time the topic was how to get more out of our students, how to help them learn more, flourish more, become more ambitious. Similarly, I held three faculty meetings per year. I spoke informally for about twenty minutes, after which we had open microphones for the 250 or so faculty members present, followed by a two-hour reception. In this larger setting a wider variety of topics tended to be raised, but even here, how to help our students develop a greater passion for the life of the mind was not an infrequent subject. That is a faculty who cares about students and about student learning. I was not surprised, therefore, when on multiple occasions alumni donors told me that they wanted to give back to the University because of a specific faculty member whose teaching was crucial for their development. The learning experience had frequently been in an area, such as poetry or political theory, that was not directly connected to the person's profession. And yet, at Notre Dame, not unlike most other colleges and universities, one finds students who are at a loss in contemplating which faculty member should write a letter of recommendation. They do not develop a relationship with any faculty member, and they are never mentored meaningfully or encouraged to develop in distinctive ways. Unfortunately, not every student has the kind of experience both graduates and faculty members tend to prize.

Yet many do. Each year one faculty member in the College of Arts and Letters is invited to give an address on teaching. In a recent address, Christian Moevs, one of Notre Dame's greatest teachers and a prizewinning Dante scholar, spoke of the divine spark that is in all students, the love teachers owe their students, and the extent to which education transforms the soul and affects the whole person:

> If you love your students, you will not waste their time and attention. If you love them, you will not bear to bore them. If you love them, you will be attentive, sensitive to what

they need, to what isn't working. They will correct you day by day, and teach you how to teach them. . . . If there's a key to my own teaching, it's Wittgenstein's great phrase, that his aim was to prevent understanding that is unaccompanied by inner change. That is the motto of my teaching. We read these texts because they see into life, into God, into the world, into us, more deeply than we do. They set a challenge to us. To meet that challenge is to grow, to change. I always say this to students, at the beginning of every course: If we're not different, if we have not changed, as a result of reading these texts, let's all just go home. We're wasting our time. Human life, human time, is too sacred to waste. . . . What is a human being? A great concentration, embodiment, reflection, of divine light and love. Sometimes disguised a little, in a slouchy form, with a baseball cap on backwards. Yet it is really divine light, the spark of divine awareness, the light of the world, that is reflected in our students' eyes. The love that moves the sun and other stars, as Dante says. There is no greater treasure. / Everyone is on a path from God, to God, in God, whether or not we are aware of it. There are advantages to being aware of it, ever more deeply aware of it. True education is an ever deeper awareness of the immanence of the divine in oneself, in others, in all things. My real job as a teacher is to live in that awareness, and to foster it in my students. Only that can change me, change them, and thus change the world.

———

One of the least controversial and most effective strategies for helping students change, for helping them develop as persons, is involvement in extracurricular activities. Liberal arts colleges are particularly adept at fostering extracurricular learning opportunities. These include student government; peer and residential advising; music ensembles; theater productions; student publications; disciplinary, political, and religious clubs; intercollegiate debate; and varsity and intramural athletics. In participating in such activities, students learn values that transcend the classroom, personal habits and social qualities that they will need after college: identifying with a higher purpose or cause, working as part of a collective, motivating others and managing a process, preparing for events with enthusiasm and energy, taking risks in pursuing goals, not shrinking away from difficult challenges, learning to perform under pressure, taking pleasure in accomplishing tasks, and taking responsibility for failures. Little is more important to a future employer than a worker's willingness to assume responsibility. College is not only about intellectual inquiry; it involves educating toward maturity and encouraging students to reach their full potential as humans in mind, body, and spirit. Discipline, self-sacrifice, teamwork, and community spirit are all fostered in extracurricular endeavors. Devotion to a cause, as it unfolds in student groups, ensures the development of practical virtues. Above all, the opportunities for leadership in student organizations allow students to experience how to inspire and organize others, how to plan various activities, and how to achieve goals.

The community service programs that are common at many liberal arts colleges and universities likewise foster broader virtues of character, such as caring for others in need, understanding their situation, becoming close to them, and helping them. Students turn the desire for kindness into action and thereby cultivate in themselves a greater awareness of the wider world and a disposition toward social responsibility. Especially useful are so-called service learning classes, where the outreach to those in need is linked with academic content. Examples would include courses on medical anthropology, the economics of poverty, Catholic social thought, or the philosophy of education that include outreach components. Or one might think of service projects that draw on disciplinary knowledge, such as analyses of lead paint in homes situated in poorer neighborhoods, energy efficiency studies for non-profit organizations, or strategies for improving literacy in local schools. In some cases, service projects integrate nicely with undergraduate research, for example, on age-based conflict resolution strategies, on the impact of Head Start on literacy and math skills, on the family situations of juvenile delinquents, or on the primary catalysts for home mortgage foreclosures.

These activities are meaningful in themselves. In some cases, they serve others, and in virtually all cases they help students develop various virtues. Activities of this kind also provide an appropriate balance: first, because the life of a college student is an intellectual one, and we all need social and physical balance; second, because college life often involves private inquiry, and students benefit from teamwork and a sense of the social world; and finally, because the life of a student is removed from the daily routine of those outside the campus environment, and that otherworldly focus can be alienating. My own time as an undergraduate involved not only meaningful activities in my residential hall and the pursuit of athletics (swimming and water polo), both of which were rewarding and memorable, but also community service. Each week I visited the local nursing home in Williamstown to spend time with elderly people who had few visitors. Those visits and the stories told to me by the residents were as memorable to me as the classes I took. I still vividly recall a resident who lamented again and again the difficulties and challenges of her life, including the tragic loss of her son. Young people are impressionable, and connections of that kind make a tremendous difference in their formation.

I also struggled with the isolation of the ivory tower. When I returned to campus for my sophomore year, I decided that I wanted to work off campus. College was too removed from real life, and I was seeking more balance. Having worked my way up, through a series of unexpected events, to head chef of a restaurant, the Humarock Lodge, the summer I turned eighteen, I decided I would walk the several miles to the various restaurants in town, offering my services as a cook. After being rebuffed at two or three restaurants, I was given a job at the Treadway Williams Inn. Several weeks later, I recognized that the work was interfering with my full experience of campus life. Recognizing that the spending money was not worth the loss of valuable time, I gave notice. It was sobering to me that one reason I was hired (and eventually offered the opportunity to work any night I wished) was that the chef did not receive any nights off; he did so only when I worked. Not only was education and the life of the mind becoming increasingly attractive to me on its own, a college degree would surely give me, I thought, a job that was less oppressive than the demands of being the only chef at a restaurant that was open seven days a week.

Living together in a community, which is essential to the identity of every residential liberal arts college, fosters emotional and social intelligence. A recent topic for modern business has been the extent to which we have different kinds of abilities and different kinds of motivations beyond the purely cognitive. Emotional intelligence, for example, signifies an ability to recognize one's own emotions, to be able to manage them in meaningful ways, to be aware of the emotions and feelings of others, and to understand how to work effectively with others, including how to inspire and motivate them. Drawing on Aristotle, Daniel Goleman suggests that our challenge is "to manage our emotional life with intelligence" (xxiv). The importance of emotional intelligence is clear for business. Goleman and his co-authors suggest: "Having a larger repertoire of emotional intelligence strengths can make a leader more effective because it means that leader is flexible enough to handle the wide-ranging demands of running an organization" (84). Social intelligence is a form of emotional intelligence and signifies the ability to be intelligent and wise in one's relations with others. It presupposes hermeneutic capacities, which are cultivated in the liberal arts: how to read situations and how to read others, including having a certain level of empathy. Social intelligence includes having the right emotions, which, insofar as emotions are contagious, serve to elevate the attitudes and contributions of others.

In a residential environment students learn to build a supportive and empathetic community with persons of very divergent backgrounds and often competing interests; they learn to understand, accept, and embrace differences and to work cooperatively despite disagreements, fostering virtues that are essential to the flourishing of a pluralistic society (Botstein 213). Moreover, the more different the students are, the more likely they are to learn from one another. Empirical research confirms that diversity contributes to good learning.[7] Robert Putnam has shown that as our world has become more diverse, our social relations and sense of trust in others have diminished. To break down the barriers of diversity, as difficult as this might be, is to open up opportunities for new bonds of empathy, trust, and solidarity. College provides these opportunities for students, both in their study abroad experiences and in daily life in the residential halls. Those students who have engaged diversity both existentially and intellectually are more likely to be able to bridge social divisions and foster more encompassing identities later in life. In a residential setting, students gain a sense for what motivates others and what strategies exist for navigating through difficult circumstances. One becomes schooled in humor and hope. Humility, gratitude, and forgiveness, discipline, loyalty, and prudence can all be tested and fostered in the context of such relationships. Moral capacities are a function not simply of reasoning but also of experience, practice, and habit. To that end, a holistic education fosters a learning environment beyond the classroom. Not surprisingly, students who live on campus not only develop as persons; they also tend to be more engaged academically (Keup and Stolzenberg 42).

————

A distinguishing characteristic of the modern age, along with the elevation of instrumental values, is the loss of an organic worldview. The modern world is characterized by a splintering of the spheres of life into autonomous subsystems, each of which is segregated from the others and each of which develops according to its own inner logic. Art, business, education law, politics, science—each is divorced from the sphere of values, which is deemed to be subjective and private. This view of modernity has been increasingly prominent in the analyses of sociologists from Max Weber to Niklas Luhmann. University functions are likewise parceled out discretely: in many cases student advising is handled by professionals, who may themselves never teach. Such advisors tend to know requirements better than faculty members, but they are rarely more equipped to help students think about larger issues, including the purpose of a liberal arts education. Yet many faculty members are inclined to address only cognition and only those issues covered by their discipline. This compartmentalization reinforces our understanding of why some scholars have become hesitant to venture beyond their autonomous spheres and why students are commonly left without guidance in their pursuit of the great questions. The linking of autonomous value systems with the purpose and organization of a university finds its most persuasive contemporary embodiment in the analyses of Stanley Fish, whose distinction may lie more in his candor and rhetoric than in the originality of his position, which bans values from the university and challenges any unifying theory of education.

Offering one of the richest analyses of the modern age, Hermann Broch discusses this concept of partial or autonomous value systems in his grand philosophical novel *The Sleepwalkers*:

> The logic of the soldier demands that he shall throw a hand-grenade between the legs of his enemy . . . the logic of the businessman demands that all commercial resources shall be exploited with the utmost rigor and efficiency to bring about the destruction of all competition and the sole domination of his own business, whether that be a trading house or a factory or a company or other economic body; /

the logic of the painter demands that the principles of painting shall be followed to their conclusion with the utmost rigor and thoroughness, at the peril of producing pictures that are completely esoteric and comprehensible only to those who produce them: . . . war is war, *l'art pour l'art,* in politics there's no room for compunction, business is business,–all these signify the same thing, all these appertain to the same aggressive and radical spirit, informed by that uncanny, I might almost say that metaphysical, lack of concern for consequences, that ruthless logic directed toward the object and the object alone, which looks neither to the right nor to the left; and this, all this, is the style of thinking that characterizes our age. (445–46, translation modified).

Partly as a consequence of the kind of mentality Broch describes, a wider consideration of formation and development of character has been increasingly neglected in the academy. Technique has displaced the overarching goal of moral formation, much as business practices or scientific advances have tended to divorce themselves from their connection to issues of values. To claim that whatever life-forms happen to exist are acceptable because moral evaluation belongs to a different realm, is itself a normative claim that invites critique. Morals, as Vittorio Hösle argues persuasively in *Morals and Politics,* do not constitute one subsystem among others, such that there is art, education, law, science, religion, business, politics, and so forth, *alongside* morals. Instead, morals are a guiding principle for all human endeavor (76–80).

In classical Greek culture and in Christian culture, moral and intellectual values functioned in tandem. What was done intellectually served a moral purpose. In the early modern period a shift occurred. In his *New Atlantis,* Francis Bacon elaborated a utopian scientific program that sought to push science to the limits of what was possible and which, through its secrecy, would have extraordinary autonomy vis-à-vis society. In the wake of this seventeenth-century development, science was no longer a form of holistic knowledge related to the metaphysical order; instead, a priori knowledge and the search for a system eventually gave way to unencumbered empirical research, often no longer, as with Bacon still, in the service of society. Later, social and economic factors contributed to this increasing autonomy. Science and technology were guided no longer by religious tradition or social custom but by the love of invention, independent of consequences, and the desire for profit. Extended into the present, this trajectory has reinforced the research focus of universities, a focus that is tied as much to external funding as it is to the discovery and dissemination of new knowledge and is almost universally disconnected from any search for the unity of truth.

Ideally, a liberal arts education seeks a more holistic model and a deeper connection to morality. Ernest Boyer has argued that today "we need educated men and women who not only pursue their own personal interests but are also prepared to fulfill their social and civic obligations. And it is during the undergraduate experience, perhaps more than at any other time, that these essential qualities of mind and character are refined" (7). *Educating Citizens*, a publication of the Carnegie Foundation for the Advancement of Teaching, which Boyer led from 1979 to 1995, has sought to redirect debate on this issue and return educators to the ideal of helping college students discover substantive values, refine personal integrity, and develop a social conscience. Anne Colby and her co-authors focus on three broad principles for preparing undergraduates to be responsible citizens: first, moral and civic understanding, which includes moral interpretation and judgment, the grasp of key concepts such as impartiality, democracy, and justice, and substantive knowledge of the diverse fields in which students might become engaged; second, moral and civic motivation, including compassion, empathy, hope, inspiration, and one's sense of moral and civic identity; and, third, core skills for transforming judgment into action and carrying out moral and civic responsibility, including interpersonal and communication skills as well as strategic intelligence (19–20, 278–79).

These three capacities—understanding moral issues in their complexity, acquiring the formal ability to realize a moral vision, and developing the identity or desire to do so—are best developed by way of a liberal arts education. Indeed, one study suggests that whereas liberal arts students make substantial advances during their college years in principled reasoning and moral judgment, students who major in business and education do not develop in the same way (McNeel 34–35 and 40–41). Another study concludes that "an increase in the number of business courses is correlated with a statistically significant decrease in political participation, voting turnout, hours of community service, and perceived importance of influencing the political structure."[8] Majoring in business has also been shown to have a negative effect on self-reported growth in cultural awareness (Astin, *What Matters* 230, 370).

A stress on education for citizenship has become a focus of the Center for Liberal Education and Civic Engagement, which is a joint effort of the Association of American Colleges and Universities and Campus Compact, itself a national coalition of colleges and universities committed to the civic purposes of higher education, including community service. Central to the connection between liberal learning and service to justice is the synergy between, on the one hand, the idea of an education that tends to the whole and, on the other hand, the obligations we have as individuals to the whole of which we are a mere part and which includes many underserved persons.

▬▬▬

    Persons want not simply to make a living but also to fulfill a higher obligation. In an exploration of the crisis of morale among American lawyers, *The Lost Lawyer,* Anthony

Kronman suggests that this crisis derives from a focus on technical expertise and advocacy at the expense of prudence and wisdom. Lawyers, he argues, center their work on the ability to persuade, with an indifference to truth and an eye toward profit, instead of on the ability to pursue truth and make judgments while appealing to ideals that transcend expediency. Kronman's distinction between the lawyer-advocate, with her focus on strategies and the importance of details in the service of profit, and the lawyer-statesman, with her focus on ends and the value of ideas in the service of the civic good, is an example of what I have in mind when I suggest that we should foster not simply formal skills to gain employment, but a calling that gives our pursuit dignity, higher meaning, and a sense of fulfillment. The "practical wisdom" that Kronman elevates is "not just a skill but a trait of character" (269). He notes, "The claim that someone has good judgment is understood to be a claim about his character and not merely the breadth of his learning or the brilliance of his mind" (16). Kronman continues,

> The ideal of the lawyer statesman was an ideal of character. This meant that as one moved toward it, one became not just an accomplished technician but a distinctive and estimable type of human being—a person of practical wisdom. And that was an ennobling thought, even for those who fell short of the ideal or found they had only limited opportunities in their own work to exercise the deliberative virtues that the lawyer-statesman exhibited to an exemplary degree. (16)

Because this ideal engages the whole person, it offers a level of fulfillment and a depth of satisfaction that is not common when one's profession is reduced to narrow technique and mere expediency. The question is not simply, which career should I pursue, but also, in what ways should I pursue the career I have chosen.

Just as declining numbers of students report substantial progress across time in "personal development," so do they report less progress in "broadening acquaintance and an enjoyment of literature" and in their "understanding and enjoyment of art, music, and theater" (Kuh, "How" 105). Through their engagement with literature, students encounter imaginative and compelling situations that they have yet to experience and which are capable of giving them a more differentiated grasp of life as well as a wider and more nuanced moral compass. Character is formed and leadership developed as much by models and the imagination as by theory and practice, and meaningful models are readily available through history and literature. Important in the mediation of such models is the encounter both with figures in one's own tradition or era and persons of great moral value from a variety of traditions, cultures, and ages.

Not only is the admiration of models awakened through literature. Also, empathy with suffering persons arises in literary works that portray the pivotal events and inner lives of others across the lines of class and gender, of nation and era. Such experiences give our students new moral perspectives, deepen their sensibilities, and expand their emotional richness. Studies of leadership have increasingly recognized that empathy is crucial for business leadership. Daniel Goleman and his co-authors argue that of all the emotional intelligence competencies, "empathy matters most to visionary leadership. The ability to sense how others feel and to understand their perspectives means that a leader can articulate a truly inspirational vision. A leader who misreads people, on the other hand, simply can't inspire them" (59).

Learning that resonates with strong existential interests or problems that students have witnessed firsthand is not only deeper, it fosters the link between learning and character.[9] For this reason alone, courses ideally address questions that already engage students or that are designed in such a way as to awaken or expand their interests. Literature that is chosen, read, or discussed with an eye to its meaning for life can also foster this goal. Not surprisingly, persons who read literature are much more likely to perform volunteer and charity work than those who do not read (*Reading at Risk* 6; *To Read* 18, 88–89).

To participate in an ideal classroom discussion of art or literature or philosophy or theology is to make connections between great questions and one's view of the world. It fosters the existential link that aids learning. Such connections are not as likely to occur in courses with a more vocational orientation. These courses will have less inner meaning and are less likely to foster wonder. Although we tend to associate the German university with a model of pure research, one of the original architects of the German university, Wilhem von Humboldt, insisted on the link between learning and character, knowledge and inner meaning: "For only scholarship that comes from within and can be planted into the inner being shapes and forms character, and the state is as little concerned, as is humanity, with knowledge and speech but with character and action" (258).

An example of an effort to connect liberal arts learning with a broader audience and to engage persons also in moral formation through discussion of great works is the World Masterpieces Seminar at the Center for the Homeless in South Bend.[10] The concept of the seminar was initiated by the Program of Liberal Studies (PLS), the great books major at the University of Notre Dame, when it asked how it might make a collective contribution to the community. Inspired by the idea that a great books education can foster human development, PLS faculty members noted that although the term "liberal arts" had originated in reference to the arts of men who had the time and privilege to explore them, in our democratic age the term has come to refer to the liberating effect of the arts and sciences, which can prepare any man or woman for full participation in a community.

In addition, as a department within a Catholic university, the Program of Liberal Studies resolved that it should in some way address the Church's "preferential option for the poor" and reach out to those at the margins of society.[11] Thus, the Program of Liberal Studies and the Center for the Homeless began to offer the World Masterpieces Seminar—short seminars in the great books, with a focus on topics such as Justice and Tyranny, Self-discovery, and God and Nature—and have done so since 1998. The success of the World Masterpieces Seminar reminds us that we impoverish ourselves when we view the choice between the practical and the intellectual as one that must favor the practical. Such an elevation can be patronizing toward persons in challenging situations when a contrary approach that awakens intellectual development can be empowering.

Participants of the World Masterpieces Seminar have found it to be helpful in different ways.[12] "Those of us in the grip of addiction use this process to rethink our lives," said Michael Newton, age fifty, originally of New York City, who had been homeless for sixteenth months. He continued, "Socrates makes clear that you have to have the courage to examine yourself and to stand up for something. A lot of us have justified our weaknesses for too long a time." Ted West, age thirty-nine, explained the value of the seminar in this way,

> When you come out of the fog of addiction, you thirst for knowledge. You feel there is so much you missed. For twenty years, I never had a goal beyond where my next glass of vodka was coming from. When Socrates talks about the pleasure of knowledge, I know exactly what he means.

He added, by way of background,

> My health was miserable, my life was failing. I was vomiting blood, I weighed 139 pounds. I was hanging around

with crazy people. I couldn't even light a cigarette, I was so shaky. It took me a couple pints of vodka to go to sleep at night. Now I need structure in my life and reading these books has become an important form of structure.

Denis Kazmierczak, age fifty-four, a former flower arranger and actor, remarked that the course has been "a sanctuary, someplace I can go where people appreciate me for my mind." He elaborated,

> It is hard to find beauty when you are in the situation we are in. But I have come to realize through the reading that in some ways everybody is homeless. You can be sitting in your fancy penthouse apartment looking out at the world but your life can be hollow. Now my mind is active, I have picked up a lost thread. Who knows? Maybe one day I'll write the great American novel.

▬▬▬

Today's age does not easily lend itself to a sense of coherence, but to read great literature and to understand the unfolding narrative of a human life, as well as the developing whole of an artwork, we gain a deeper sense of coherence that is transferable to reflection on our selves, on the hidden logic of our own development. The meaning of literature for life—both the refinement of the reader's formal capacities and the enrichment of self through its meanings—is not unrelated to a full understanding of hermeneutics. An important dimension of hermeneutics beyond the concepts of understanding (*subtilitas intelligendi*) and interpretation (*subtilitas explicandi*) is application (*subtilitas applicandi*). In jurisprudence, the meaning of the law is not a dry lesson in interpretation but has consequences for individual cases; in theology, the scriptures are not explicated simply as historical documents but are to be read for spiritual edification, with an eye to their relevance for life, made apparent in the explication of the homily. Within literary studies, historicism and value-free science have led to considerable neglect of this important hermeneutic principle.

The eminent University of Chicago philosopher Martha Nussbaum tells the moving story of her transition to graduate studies at Harvard, where neither the department of philosophy nor the department of classics would engage the great questions that arose in Greek literature about how we should live and what literary forms can best express those ideals (*Love's Knowledge* 10–23). She is surely not alone. Many an undergraduate chooses graduate study out of a love of literature and a love of the great questions but finds instead a focus on parochial debates and overly narrow inquiries. If we are to meet our highest calling and entice students, the question, "What does a literary work tell us about life?" must remain in the forefront of our concerns. Without this integrative moment, the study of literature loses its existential value and higher meaning. However refined the intellectual gymnastics of our interpretive efforts might be, they are complete only when a bridge is drawn to the existential sphere. When students do connect with a work in this way, they learn immeasurably more.

One of my first papers as an undergraduate was on Homer. Having been raised a Catholic, I read Homer's two epics with amazement. On the one hand, there was no doubt, even for my limited sensibilities, of the extraordinary beauty of the pages, the engaging similes, the drama, the fascinating flashbacks, the complexity of human emotions, and the depth of relations. Also the transformation of Achilles and the cleverness of Odysseus intrigued me. On the other hand, I was openly critical of a worldview that seemed to glorify performance in battle; that understood honor only as public honor, as possessions, power, and recognition by others; and that defined excellence not by Christian virtues but by heroic valor, stubbornness, and revenge. It was a myth that I found unacceptable, and I spelled out my concerns in the paper. The teacher kindly took me aside and opened my eyes to the idea of understanding another culture on its own terms, recognizing the different mores and the other culture's animating vision of itself, its distinctive ideas of human excellence and nobility. It was an entirely new concept to me and opened another world, as it were. Sometimes existential engagement means overcoming one's own particularity to see something entirely different.

Great literature opens new horizons for students. Every such work belongs to a tradition that it invokes, reworks, or overcomes. Studying past works is an immersion in times that transcend our own. If we recognize the achievements of prior eras and the possibilities of coming generations, then one of our duties is to sift through the works of the past, to preserve them in their integrity and with the richest possible interpretations. In meaningfully preserving great literature, we exhibit respect for the past, for the originators of the works and the traditions that cultivated their interpretations, and for future persons who will likewise participate in the wonder of these works and benefit from the richest readings they have garnered. In this sense a liberal arts education evokes not only a synchronic holism of the diverse spheres of knowledge but also a diachronic holism across time.

The literature and philosophy of earlier eras can teach us specific virtues that have been neglected in the present but which represent alternatives to the contemporary world. Certain virtues are more prominent in given historical circumstances than in others. Reading older works reminds us of virtues that are less visible today but still of great value. Rare today, for example, is an indifference to one's economic position or status within society, an ability to remain autonomous, as we find in Augustine's *Confessions* or Boethius's *Consolation of Philosophy*. The elevation of instrumental reason leads many to think of grace as antiquated. Loyalty is less visible—partly because we have become so mobile, partly because our relationships have become increasingly driven by utility. Similar factors contribute to the erosion of hospitality and generosity. Physical courage is less tested in an era of due process, and civil courage, risking one's position or respect among one's peers for the sake of one's principles, also diminishes in an age that tends to place greater value on strategies and success.

Furthering our knowledge of the past is an ideal way to obtain distance from the cliches and biases of the present. An encounter with the works of other ages gives us different perspectives and alternatives to what we see on a daily basis. In that sense it can become contemporary, by which I mean here meaningful for the present, precisely because it is not contemporary, that is, of the present. Familiarity with another culture creates a critical distance toward one's own. The stories and ideas of the past and of other cultures free students from the tyranny of the local, much as identification with fictional characters takes readers beyond themselves. Their relation to the past and to the other gives them not only alternatives to motivate critique but also impulses to help them expand their identity.

Great works, as Chekhov shows in his story "The Student," address themes of universal interest. On a cold, gloomy, and windy Good Friday, a student retells the Gospel story of Peter's anguish at having betrayed Christ. The widows who listen to the story are moved, and the student has a revelation: "it was evident that what he had just been telling them about, which had happened nineteen centuries ago, had a relation to the present—to both women, to the desolate village, to himself, to all people" (108). He senses that the chain of meaning is not broken between the past and the present. This connection, which is enchanting and full of lofty meaning, gives the student in his desolate material condition a sense of great joy: "he thought that truth and beauty, which had guided human life there in the garden and in the yard of the high priest had continued without interruption to this day, and had evidently always been the chief thing in human life and in all earthly life, indeed" (108).

Through literature we learn from the past, thus rendering otherness not just an object of curiosity but a partner of existential import. By showing us what is great in the past, literature is able to remind us of what is lost with certain forms of progress and to draw our attention to values that might yet be regained. This goal can be met only if we recognize, beyond obvious historical differences, certain supertemporal constants so that our engagement with works from earlier eras is not merely antiquarian but an earnest effort to learn from those works. To have such an encounter with the past is both humbling and enriching for the present. It is to recognize that the great questions of life endure and come alive in our conversations with great works. Of course, great works are not limited to earlier eras, and as tradition evolves, new works that address topics unique to our age invite our students' attention for other reasons.

The exposure to great works and their interpretation gives students an opportunity to develop their own sense of values, to explore issues of character and motivation and complexity, to see the consequences of certain kinds of action. Such a course of study is essential to the development of the kinds of interpersonal capacities demanded in the world beyond college. Not only intellectual virtues, but also the virtues of character and leadership that are fostered through exposure to the liberal arts, are essential for business and the practical world: internal motivation and a sense of ambition, a capacity to understand others and to work with them, a sense of integrity and a desire to do good in the world.

—

Liberal arts students identify with their colleges long after they have graduated. Why? They know that the value of what they learned there far exceeds whatever tuition may have been paid, and so they graciously and generously give back to the institution, creating a bond across generations and making possible a similar experience for others. The extent of our recollection is proportional not to the amount of time we pursued a given activity but to its deeper meaning for ourselves as persons. Liberal arts graduates often reflect back on their college years because they were a time of tremendous formation, of depth of meaning pursued in a truly nurturing environment. "Much more than as a stepping stone to later careers, the alma mater is a continuing affective focus for many Americans" (Knox et al. 175). Individual identity is partly formed by our connection to collective identity, to values that transcend the individual. The common experience of a given college, with its campus traditions, rituals, special experiences, and distinctive ethos, helps form a student's sense of collective identity, and, not unrelated, students identify with the institution's highest values, which point toward transcendent meaning and encourage them to aspire to their highest potential.

Colleges have a continuing effect on students after they graduate, keeping alive in them a flame of idealism and a distinctive vision of higher purpose, helping them become ever more mature in character as well as intellect (Heath). Colleges have, therefore, a calling to embody the highest moral values in their policies and actions; they must be models for students because everything that touches a college student is a potential source of education and edification. A contemporary example would be how a college addresses the ecological crisis. A decision to pursue strategies of environmental stewardship, setting goals for the reduction of carbon emissions or even the goal of becoming carbon neutral, can have a huge impact on the consciousness of students, what they themselves think and value, and what they think of their institution.

To identify with a liberal arts college is above all to identify with the values of intellection and higher meaning that are at the core of its mission. That experience, in turn, prepares a student for identifying with the mission of her work and the sense of belonging to a common effort that is a necessary condition for any collective flourishing. Not surprisingly, in a survey of

CEOs the sixth most important quality out of sixty-three qualities identified was "motivation and commitment to the firm . . . to give 110 percent" (Harper). Identification with the collective purpose of an admirable business is similar to identification with the collective purpose of a distinctive college. The leader of such a business must articulate a vision that fosters motivation and commitment, a sense of higher meaning and purpose. Such a leader must be more than a technocrat; she must have a sense of the whole, an understanding of an institution's higher purpose, and an inspiring capacity to present its vision. Although I stressed above the pragmatic value of intellectual virtues, a desire to identify with a higher purpose is no less important, given the almost universal focus on core values.

—————

The liberal arts give students many of the human qualities sought by businesses, but even more importantly, they develop in students the capacity to ask questions about what is important in the world, who they are, and what they wish to do with their lives. To cultivate a sense of character, of purpose, of vocation, by reflecting on the world as it is and as it should be, is to unleash a passion and devotion that, much like other liberal arts capacities, will not only help students succeed in the world of work but also guide them in terms of values and life decisions.

4

Integrating the Values
of the Liberal Arts

The idea of participation in a higher reality, a connection to the transcendent, is for the most part forgotten in contemporary culture, but it is common to both a liberal arts education's intrinsic value and its cultivation of a sense of vocation, of identity and purpose. Society has an interest in colleges and universities as institutions of formation because vocation and responsibility are not simply private matters; they involve an act of reaching out toward a larger whole. Investing in educating promising students at liberal arts colleges, or at other institutions that celebrate learning opportunities commonly associated with a liberal arts education, enables the development of young persons who are likely to have a leavening effect on the larger society, which needs talented, well-developed, and moral leaders. Students enrich both themselves and others when they subordinate their particular interests to a larger and more meaningful whole. For individual identity to be rich and meaningful, it must integrate an element of collective identity, and it must attend not only to the supertemporal but also to the specific challenges of the day. The liberal arts goal of helping students understand holistically is an excellent context for this discernment process.

To make a difference in the world, to move from individual virtue to civic virtue, to transform our job or career or life into a vocation, we must recognize a set of overarching aspirations and normative ideals with which we are willing to align ourselves, and we must discern what issues in the contemporary world are most significant in light of their deviation from these higher values or in light of their pressing importance for humankind. Students must have a sense of normative goals and must understand the world sufficiently, both locally and globally, to grasp in what ways it is less than it should be. Further, they must have a sense of their own capacities. What formal skills have I developed? What moves and motivates me? We must then seek to align our talents and disposition with these recognized needs so as to serve a higher purpose. The articulation of a higher purpose, the discernment of contemporary problems, the awareness of our own capacities, and the integration of these realms are well-served by the breadth as well as the social and existential significance of a liberal arts education. What is of greatest value? What are the most pressing challenges of the age? Who am I? What ought I do with my life? These questions form the core of a liberal arts education.

▬▬▬

The intrinsic value and first purpose of a liberal arts education, as I have tried to articulate it, can be associated with the value of the lost art of contemplation, with what the Greeks called *theoria,* which is independent of practical aims. The cultivation of critical thinking and of those formal virtues that allow us to impact the world, competencies that I have explicated as the second purpose of a liberal arts education, correlates with today's elevation of science, capitalism, and technology and so can be associated with the contemporary ascendency of *poiesis* (production). The third purpose of the liberal arts, the call to virtue and vocation, mirrors to some degree the third mode of relating to the world recognized by the Greeks, *praxis* (action); this connection is present even when one's vocation may involve *theoria* as with a faculty member, or *poiesis*, as with an engineer. All of us are engaged in *praxis*, but in its richest form, *praxis* involves not only an awareness of higher values and the development of formal capacities in our relations with others but also an existential commitment, a calling to serve others in addition to ourselves. The threefold value of a liberal arts education involves an experience of intrinsic value, the development of formal skills and capacities, and a recognition of greater purpose and service to others, including a modest overestimation of one's abilities, with the recognition that one must stretch to reach one's full potential. In this sense we can view the three purposes, in another light, as the combination of knowledge, action, and love.

The first purpose is associated with understanding the world and developing a longing for truth and a hunger for transcendent principles. The second involves intellectual discipline, the ability to think creatively, systematically, and fairly and the capacity to communicate with what Jacques Barzun calls "articulate precision" (17). The third is in many respects a synthesis of the first two, for it involves both contemplation of the world and the skills of intellectual discipline to pursue an endeavor that binds us to a higher purpose. We employ our intellectual capacities for a reason that is greater than ourselves. Contemplation, which derives from the Latin *contemplare*, is associated not simply with attentive consideration but with looking for meaning or purpose. The third purpose unites the first two in another way, for by linking our activity in the world to a higher objective, we sacrifice our own interests for others. This sacrifice, or gift of one's capacities in order to help others, is useful for humanity and of intrinsic value—insofar as the very act of serving others has no higher purpose than to link a person with what confers dignity on her actions.

When I was asked to serve as a dean, my intention was not to become a career administrator, essentially giving up my first love of teaching and scholarship to help lead an institution. I accepted the role and stayed in it for more than a decade because I fell in love with Notre Dame's distinctive vision and ethos and with the University's community and aspirations. What motivated me was the identification with a higher purpose, helping an appealing but still striving institution reach a level of distinction, in the twofold sense of eminence and singularity, and taking joy in the success of others, whom I was privileged to serve. There is no pay that can compensate for the time one devotes to such a calling. One can only assume such a role and persevere in it because one identifies with the goal of fostering learning, scholarship, and formation and one recognizes the potential to impact the world more deeply in a position of leadership, even if at some level the impact is less embodied and more abstract than when working with many students and writing or researching full-time.

In my final semester as dean, the graduating seniors I had taught in their sophomore year asked for a capstone course, which I eventually agreed to offer under the title Great Questions and the Liberal Arts. It was an exploration of great questions that drew on their earlier College Seminar, coupled with meta-reflections on the value of the liberal arts, an exercise appropriate for students completing their liberal arts education. In one session, the two students leading the discussion organized a debate on the following statement, "A liberal arts education can be defended first and foremost as an end in itself." Because this discussion took place at a Catholic university, the students began to formulate their arguments with reference to God. One side argued that the ultimate end of education is to come closer to a vision of God. God, the students argued, is not found in the practical endeavor of ensuring, for example, that one can afford a larger house; God is instead an intellectual goal and is to be found in contemplation of the highest truths. The other side conceded that, while the intrinsic value of a liberal arts education leads students toward God, the intellectual and practical virtues we develop during this quest allow us to see God not merely as knowledge but also as love. That is, although thought might be its own end, in a Christian context, we experience God most fully in community. Therefore, the kind of work that results when the virtues of the liberal arts are placed in service to the larger community, addressing the needs of the age, is also a fulfillment of the idea of God as the highest end, here understood in the framework of God is love.

———

To obtain a position, to have enough money to satisfy basic needs for food and shelter, for health and safety, and for opportunities for one's children, is important, but to focus on getting a high-paying job over developing a life vision is to cut short one of the few opportunities that students have, beyond the home, to develop values and a worldview that will help them flourish as persons. Much as traditional wisdom on learning principles has now been substantiated by empirical research, so has empirical research verified the ancient wisdom that a focus on material goods and wealth beyond a basic level is harmful to the soul. Psychological research has shown that persons who are more materialistic, focusing their time and effort on accumulating wealth rather than on enacting social values, are less happy. That is, a reverse connection exists between materialistic priorities and progress toward materialistic goals, on the one hand, and emotional well being and psychological health, on the other hand. People "who strongly value the pursuit of wealth and possessions report lower psychological well-being than those who are less concerned with such aims" (Kasser 4). The focus on the spiral of ever more success, replete with praise, rewards, status, and continuing comparison with others, increases one's sense of insecurity, whereas a life focused on intrinsic value—on developing one's capacities and meeting meaningful challenges, exploring ideas, deepening friendships, fostering community—tends to increase one's sense of contentment. Empirical research suggests that the "greatest happiness comes from absorbing yourself in some goal outside yourself" (Layard 74).

The claim that a liberal arts education should not be chosen because one might not be able to have a certain level of financial success can be challenged not only in terms of the financial success liberal arts graduates can obtain but also in terms of the question of whether financial success is an appropriate measure of well being. A student recently suggested to me that his parents wanted, as a whole, to have a better life, especially materially, than did their parents, both for their own sake and for the sake of their children. They succeeded, he said, but that is not his goal. The question of what we should do with our lives, he added, becomes both more engaging and more rewarding when one becomes disillusioned with the continuous desire to out-do the previous generation in material prosperity.

Even if my second chapter, on the practicality of a liberal arts education for future employment and leadership opportunities, may resonate the most with students and their parents, it is important to remember that it is not the only rationale for having such an education. If we reduce the purpose of education to that of getting a job, we have failed to adorn it with higher meaning. The market economy by itself does not give us the higher purpose or rationale, the clarity of vision or compelling narrative, that would warrant the level of dedication we provide, as students, faculty, and supporters, to the purpose of education. Students of course want to get a job and make a living, but they also want to be able to say why the life they have chosen makes sense, in what way it is connected to something higher, above and beyond simply earning money. One wants to find something that is absorbing and challenging and at the same time will make a difference for others. Work can become an opportunity to fulfill one's potential and develop one's talents by making a difference in the world. People who feel called in this way as opposed to simply pursuing a career "score higher on job satisfaction, are more likely to say their work is meaningful, and are more likely to say it is important to them to do well in their jobs" (Wuthnow 73). Even more than awakening a deeper meaning in work, a liberal arts education gives graduates a direction for life.

The level of higher purpose in our work can be recognized in the ways in which we engage that work on a daily basis. If we have a deep sense of commitment to a cause, an objective purpose, we are unlikely to be oriented toward personal success, to desire to stand in the foreground, to concern ourselves more with external rewards and impressions than with just and responsible outcomes. We identify with the cause and are willing to sacrifice for that higher purpose. As Max Weber notes in "Politics as a Vocation," the combination of "devotion to a cause" and "distance towards one's self" provides a framework that lessens our tendency toward "vulgar vanity" and "personal self-intoxication" (116). Because we are fallible beings, we are always tempted by vanity, but the identification with a larger purpose can give us a framework that limits such expressions of insecurity. In this sense, developing a purpose or sense of vocation not only draws on intellectual and emotional elements of the self; to the extent that we are successful in identifying with a worthy cause instead of focusing on our own desire for recognition, this very attitude cultivates emotional virtues. Finally, such behavior is most likely to inspire and motivate others, subordinates and colleagues alike, as they, too, seek to pursue a vision that has intrinsic value.

The temptation to work for worldly recognition or reward, thereby reducing purpose to "eagerness of praise and desire of glory," to borrow a phrase from Augustine, is that we will do only what the consensus wants, whatever is defined by local opinion and the ruling ideology, instead of elevating the age or our surroundings (*City of God* V.12). If excellence is only revealed by praise, we are discouraged from ever challenging the views of others. In this sense and in the midst of praise, complacency wins out over aspiration, higher purpose, and courage. This is yet another reason for a strong vision and sense of purpose, which are resistant to the temptation we share as human beings toward external approbation and toward adjusting to the status quo. In this sense purpose helps to form character.

What is fascinating about developing a sense of purpose is that while purpose must originate from some level of self-knowledge (what motivates me and what am I capable of contributing?) once we identify it and begin the challenge of meeting our ambitions, we tend to forget ourselves and to devote ourselves fully to that purpose. Our private identity becomes enriched by that higher purpose. William Damon writes,

> People with purpose stop thinking about themselves, becoming fascinated instead by the work or problem at hand. As they muster their mental and physical capacities to reach a solution, they may discover powers that they never thought they had: untried talents, new skills, reservoirs of untapped energy. They feel a surge of excitement as they move toward their objective. They lose track of everyday cares and woes, of where they happen to be, of what time it is—in short, of all the mental boundaries usually posed by our physical and material worlds. (32)

We completely lose ourselves in the purpose of our vocation; this is uncannily similar to the loss of self I noted earlier when we are absorbed in reading a great work. Both are characterized by doing something as an end in itself instead of as a means to yet some other purpose.

■■■■■

While one hopes that liberal arts students will find not only employment, but purposeful employment after graduation, for those graduates who lack a deeper satisfaction in their work, the question arises, what avenues exist to escape the disenchantment that results from an emptying out of the value of work? One can initially try to reconfigure one's position or firm. If necessary, one can leave and seek other employment. Alternative employment should be a possibility for a liberal arts graduate whose background includes versatility. But when, if for whatever reason, those avenues are closed, what can one do? Here, too, the liberal arts graduate has resources on which to draw, as the liberal arts seek to cultivate a love for the life of the mind that can flourish not only on the job but also beyond one's occupation. If work becomes simply a means to make a living, the liberal arts graduate should be able to find purpose in other realms, beyond work. Such a graduate has more resources at her disposal than someone whose education found its purpose in mastering the technical aspects of a given profession.

Not only those whose gainful employment is without higher meaning but also those whose work is not in the marketplace can draw on their liberal arts background to help them find higher meaning. For example, some liberal arts graduates will choose to stay home to raise their children while a spouse earns an income. Meaning can occur in the family and in the realm of thought and ideas. It can also be found in more public settings, by playing a participatory or leadership role in a local community organization, a social movement, or a political institution or by becoming an informal voice in public affairs by writing letters to political figures and newspapers or even by writing essays for newspapers and magazines. This is indeed a very American ideal, as it was Thomas Jefferson who argued that "liberal education" is "the most effectual means" for citizens who want to ensure that their government does not abuse power and that its leaders do not have ambitions for themselves at the expense of "the rights and liberties of their fellow citizens" (235–36). To identify with a higher purpose is to have a reservoir of emotional strength that could be said to match and enhance the reservoir of learning on which the liberal arts graduate can draw; both are healthy for the self. William Damon notes, "Purpose endows a person with joy in good times and resilience in hard times, and this holds true all throughout life" (31).

While every liberal arts graduate will have experienced all three dimensions of a liberal education—the intrinsic, the practical, and the idealistic—graduates may be especially drawn by internal inclination or external opportunity to one dimension or another. A certain percentage of them will pursue the life of the mind, becoming artists, scientists, scholars, or teachers. Many will draw on their formal capacities and enter mainstream professions in business, law, medicine, and public service. And some will take an unusual path, pursuing distinctive opportunities as diverse as foreign correspondent, social activist, forest ranger, or minister. Many will combine all three dimensions, in some cases over time and in other instances simultaneously, be it in their professional lives or in a combination of their personal and professional lives. One of the great aspects of the liberal arts is that one never leaves that world behind, and so all three dimensions are in some manner ever present, even if in submerged ways. Another way of understanding this point is by recognizing that the life-long desire for learning that is cultivated as a formal skill helps graduates as they discern, over time, that their vocation and sense of purpose may well develop in unexpected directions.

In the end, a liberal arts education is useful in all three respects discussed here. First, it addresses our highest ends, what is of value for its own sake, useless for other purposes but useful in itself. The concept of what is an end in itself shatters a narrow concept of the useful as simply the means to an end. The useful is not one and the same with the good. Second, a liberal arts education undermines a false concept of the useful as what is only immediately applicable. Such an education helps students develop formal skills that will allow them to flourish, whatever career paths they might choose or life choices they might make over time; indeed, many of the skills they develop will reveal their significance only later in life. Third, a liberal arts education helps develop character. As Thomas Jefferson notes, "everything is useful which contributes to fix in the principles and practices of virtue" (233). Such an education encourages reflection on the highest possible ends to which students might put their formal capacities and so helps them discover how their learning might be most meaningfully and usefully employed. A liberal arts education does not simply give students a capacity for clear and persuasive speech; it helps them discover the purposes to which such speech should be used. The notion of the useful as that which involves a short-term goal, that is, getting a career, is here superseded by the higher concept of reflecting on a worthy purpose, what students are called to do in their lives. Liberal thinking, with the goal of criticizing inadequate positions in the status quo and developing ideas for change, is intimately related to the ideal of forming "a better world" (Shapiro 71).

Just as the time outside the classroom also represents the joy of discovering oneself and the world as well as the development of one's capacities for interpersonal relations and for listening and speaking, so, too, is one's sense of higher purpose cultivated beyond the classroom. Student conversations in residential halls represent a further opportunity to ask life's greater questions, and while these will in most cases emerge on their own, educators can seek ways to cultivate discussions by fostering student-faculty contact and fora on enduring questions, the central issues of the age, and the challenges of discerning a vocation. These topics often transcend the focused disciplinary discourse that guides much of the learning and scholarship at the nation's leading universities.

———

To develop a vocation, an ultimate concern or animating purpose, is to ask the question, how does the world as it is differ from how it should be. This requires, on the one hand, a capacity to articulate an ideal and a command of transcendental categories, and, on the other hand, an ability to discern reality in its complexity, a sensibility for what is. To ask such far-reaching questions is to escape simple patterns of thought and to push our thinking into creative and entirely new territory. It requires engagement with great questions and so affords students the opportunity to transcend the frequent cultural focus on short-term, trivial, and materialistic goals and to develop a nobler sense of vocation that will answer their innate idealistic tendencies. This knowledge of the transcendent and of the world must be combined with self-knowledge, knowledge of what one can do and what generates one's enthusiasm and interest. Identification of a role or purpose is to unite what *should* be with what we *want* to do. In this sense, forming character and discerning a vocation, the topics of chapters three and four, integrate chapter one (engaging such great questions as, how does the world differ from how it should be?) and chapter two (developing formal capacities in students that will allow them eventually to play a role in bridging that difference).

Self-awareness is essential both to discovering what motivates us, wherein we experience pleasure, and to recognizing what kinds of roles we can fulfill. Also, as individuals, we need to comprehend our unique constellation of capacities and interests. What do I care most about in the world today? What can I bring to an issue that no one else can? What role can I contribute within a much larger context? Because self-knowledge has both intellectual and emotional dimensions, we ask not only what capacities have we developed, but also what capacities do we enjoy exercising. For a student, these formative questions transcend one's academic major and ask, Do I prefer to employ analytical, quantitative, interpersonal, language, or creative skills? Do I want to create a business, address social problems, provide a service to the community, or do something else altogether? Increasingly, in our complex world graduates will choose across their career life both a variety of capacities and an array of career paths.

In seeking to make a positive difference in the world, students must find a part to play that is neither too ambitious (and which they cannot fulfill) nor too modest (and which could lead to boredom for them and untapped potential, which could have made a difference for themselves and others). Of course, as with tough grading that encourages students to extend themselves, so in the discernment of our life goals, we need to stretch to some degree. Challenges and opportunities bring out virtues of which we were previously unaware. Thus, Weber proposes "that the human being would not have attained the possible unless time and again he had not reached out for the impossible" ("Politics" 128, translation modified). Discerning and realizing a vocation involves more than posing questions and exploring intellectual and existential puzzles. To bridge the gap between one's learning and the world, indeed, to further one's learning and make a positive difference in the world, one must work with others to help lift a community. One needs not only insight but also constructive cooperation with others.

One of the fascinating aspects of the communal dimensions and collective passions of college life is that they complement, in appealing ways, the intellectual vocation that students develop. What do I mean by this? Intellectuals develop the capacity to question everything, not only the positions of others, but also their own positions and the easy certainties and half-truths of their own institution or firm, their own background or nation (Said). The intellectual's highest allegiance is not to an embodied institution but to universal ideals of truth and justice that may call into question the current policies of existing institutions and alert us to the gaps between how an institution is and how it should be. To be less than fully at home, less than fully settled, where one is, marks the life of an intellectual, but to understand that such a disjunction is a necessary condition of progress is, at a higher level, to be at home in the world as process. The affirmation of higher ideals, in their contrast to embodied institutions, is necessary to ensure the improvement of existing institutions and so can be viewed as identification with the institution in its higher potentiality. In this sense, criticism can be a kind of solidarity, and in the case of a nation, a form of patriotism.

When students return from abroad, from that distinctive learning experience in which the external world becomes a kind of classroom, they often despair of the weaknesses in their own country, which become visible to them in unprecedented ways. The most appropriate and productive response is to turn that unease into hope. That means asking the question, how might the student contribute to improving her country? This transformation from despair to hope can be accomplished more easily when students have opportunities to discuss with others not only their scholarly development but also their existential concerns.

In a sense, the experience of returning from abroad is a microcosm of the alienation that takes place in any student who goes away to college. A challenge for every liberal arts student, and a reason why some parents do not want their children to attend college or to attend college away from home, is that as the student gains distance from the everyday and encounters new ideas and positions, a moment of partial alienation from one's past becomes inevitable. Not by chance Hegel entitled a section of his *Phenomenology of Spirit*, "Self-Alienated Spirit. Education" (3: 359). William Torrey Harris, the U.S. Commissioner of Education from 1889 to 1906, himself a Hegelian, viewed "self-estrangement" as "perhaps the most important idea in the philosophy of education" (27). The recent *Report of the Task Force on General Education* by Harvard University also stresses "alienation," arguing that "the aim of a liberal education is to unsettle presumptions, to defamiliarize the familiar, to reveal what is going on beneath and behind appearances, to disorient young people and to help them find ways to reorient themselves" (1–2).

The critical lens that allows educated persons to see weaknesses in the present that were previously not visible to them ensures a moment of distance to the present that will carry forward beyond the college experience and is not without its costs. The alienation and, in a sense, disappointment, that comes from developing such a critical perspective can lead to an identity crisis, but such a crisis is also the first condition for a richer and more profound identity (Hösle, "Crises of Identity"). Such distance is also a prerequisite for progress and for work that seeks to improve on the deficiencies of the present. To gain distance from oneself and one's surroundings is essential to self-reflection, self-awareness, education.

Criticism represents a potential tension, in one's affective relation to one's time and place and in the reception of one's critical comments. To note weaknesses not only in other countries, including countries with whom we are at war is easy; to note weaknesses in one's own country, when it is engaged in war, is to invite criticism of oneself. To speak and to hear such tension is a mark of progress, and an intellectual learns to be receptive to discussion of such disjunctions, indeed to initiate such discussions. To express criticism both diplomatically and courageously, with an eye toward progress, and not to fall backward into smug and self-righteous critique, is a moral value. Similarly, to be able to hear criticism of one's nation, firm, or institution or of oneself, not as mere critique but as a gift that can help foster success at a higher level, is a virtue. To work within such parameters is not easy, but to have explored such situations in the liberal arts disciplines, which are replete with examples in literature, history, and the social sciences, can help students grow toward this ideal. No less important in such a context is the emotional intelligence to know what can and cannot be changed, so that one is not bitter or cynical, but content with the present, even as one seeks to improve it. It is important for students who struggle with such issues to have a supportive environment for such intellectual and emotional challenges. Because parents are not the most obvious outlets for such tensions, it is important that interlocutors be found among other students, among residential advisors, and, to some extent, among the very faculty members whose courses may have contributed to the students' alienation.

It is also essential for firms to recognize that at appropriate times what they most need to hear in order to improve is what is not working well. To that end, leaders need to have the courage to hire liberal arts graduates, at least those who have critical thinking skills along with a combination of honesty and diplomacy. When I was a graduate student at Princeton and my wife worked on Wall Street, the word in her firm was never to hire a Ph.D. Doctorates, she had been told, have a reputation for narrowness and arrogance and are rarely seen as team players. The firm did not feel the same way about liberal arts graduates, whose most recent education included both intellectual and social components and who were more in touch with what they did not yet know. In that, they knew more.

Whereas the first value of the liberal arts could be said to focus on content, what questions are important and what students should know in the diverse disciplines, the second involves the development of students' capacities, the formal aspects of education. Many see the end of education in knowledge of content, mastery of a certain set of ideas or works, exposure to the appropriate material of a discipline. Others define the purpose of education as the development of formal capacities and intellectual skills—writing, quantitative reasoning, and so forth. Those who believe that education is about the knowledge of specific content do not always agree with one another. If we are to teach students about civil society, for example, should they take courses in the great books of the Western tradition, which offer insights into founding principles, or should they focus on contemporary problems and issues, which allow them to understand arguments concerning the basic topics of our age, such as the challenges of developing countries, race and gender issues, or the ecological question?

My response to these two dilemmas, first between content and form and then concerning which kind of content, is that students need, in some way or another, each of these approaches, along with a third, what I call the existential component. The existential dimension of education can be layered into each option, as the great questions do give meaning, contemporary issues have obvious existential resonance, and the development of formal skills has significance for students' futures. Students want to learn not only *about* a subject; they also want to learn *from* a subject.

Students benefit from encounters with the tradition, especially because some of the great questions asked by earlier thinkers tend to be neglected over time and because the knowledge of other ages and other cultures is one of the best strategies to recognize alternatives to one's own worldview and those of our time and place. But this cannot be undertaken in an antiquarian way; the issues must be shown to have relevance for value questions that engage the students today. Students, for example, learn more when they are allowed to formulate their own seminar paper topics and explore themes that are of particular significance to them, about which they have developed a personal curiosity; such choices need to be made within parameters that are appropriate for the course. One of my colleagues in the department of history at Notre Dame requires papers with only three guidelines: the paper must relate to the general theme of the class, it must utilize primary research, and the professor must approve the topic. Within that broad frame, students can be creative and can develop a topic that they find personally compelling. We need to link the established content and methods of the disciplines with questions that truly engage students and help them develop as intellectuals and as persons. A course on the ancient world will appeal to students more when they see that the questions asked by characters in Plato's dialogues and Sophocles' dramas still have meaning and resonance today. And a course on econometrics or on quantitative analysis will be more positively received when a connection is drawn to issues that the student recognizes as significant today. Often a choice needs to be rethought in its exclusivity.

Yet such decisions do not always come easily. At Notre Dame, we discussed at more than ten faculty meetings, beginning before I became dean and ending some six years later, what to do about our so-called core course, which lacked both student and faculty support, but could not easily be abandoned without some loss to the students. We solved the impasse, I believe, by focusing on three questions: First, how do we define an educated person today, especially a liberal arts graduate of a Catholic university? What characteristics does such a person have? Second, what are the greatest gaps our students have today? What are their most glaring weaknesses? Finally, what courses will help students approximate our educational ideal and overcome their existing weaknesses? By focusing on an educational ideal and on our students' current gaps, we were able to take off the table the entrenched disciplinary interests that sometimes drive curricular discussions. We settled on the abovementioned College Seminar, which addresses great questions but also focuses on those formal skills that we thought students most needed to develop.

———

Not only students and their parents, but also faculty members, who might themselves become all too easily absorbed in the fascinating details of their own subjects, need to be reminded of the distinctive values and opportunities of a liberal education. Learning goals, which are central to every college course, should address not only the specific content and methodology of the course but also the ways in which the course satisfies our intrinsic desire for knowledge and the joy of discovery. In rushing to specific content, faculty members sometimes forget to include a learning goal that addresses the value of learning for its own sake. Learning goals on course syllabi should spell out, among other things, that students will gain familiarity with a fascinating question appropriate for emerging intellectuals and, in so doing, will learn to enjoy the life of the mind and to grasp the value of wonder and mystery. To help students achieve such a celebration of the life of the mind, the teacher must express in the classroom and beyond a love of the subject that is not one and the same with scholarly competency or command of the material. In this, faculty members must be more than mere academics; they must be intellectuals and lovers of wisdom.

Whatever discipline one is teaching, the development of formal skills should be highlighted as learning goals or outcomes. Faculty members might state that students will learn the diversity of ways in which several disciplines approach a challenging issue; that students will advance their skills in evaluating the tenability of various kinds of arguments; that they will develop felicity in making arguments with the help of quantitative evidence; that they will develop their capacity to interpret cultural documents, for example, by asking pertinent and interesting questions of works and arguing for and against various interpretations; that they will learn to become more adept in intellectual discussion, improving their capacity for empathetic and thoughtful listening as well as for precision of speech and persuasive argument; that they will discover how much they are able to learn from one another; that they will advance in their mastery of the English language, both spoken and written, including their sense of style; or that they will improve their basic communication skills insofar as they accompany the organization and communication of their thoughts. By introducing learning goals along these lines, a faculty member can encourage meta-reflection on the methods of a discipline as useful beyond the discipline itself and so help students feel comfortable taking a course for the love of the material, all the while knowing that they are gaining the skills that will allow them to flourish beyond the classroom.

Very important is to extend learning goals also toward the transcendent, by opening a window onto the existential and higher purpose of a given discipline and the questions it pursues. An example would be a set of statements such as the following: Students will develop their own positions on the topic of the course, and they will be able to describe them and defend them in the light of alternative positions. At the same time, they will become more conscious of the mysterious and inexhaustible nature of the subject matter. In relating to these issues in a personal way, students will recognize a strong relationship between their academic work and their personal lives, developing in the process a sense of the meaning of the material for their life goals and values. A history class might include as one goal among many helping students understand how various historical figures set priorities or dealt with problems and crises. Such a goal has intrinsic value, helps sharpen students' capacities for interpretation and evaluation, and aids them, indirectly, as they seek to develop themselves as persons who will similarly have to set priorities and deal with problems. A science class might stress some of the virtues of character, such as honesty and integrity, discipline and perseverance, modesty and teamwork, that will be developed in the course of exploring a topic as part of a research team. Or a course goal might note that students will see a connection between the scientific principles explored and questions of public policy.

While not every course will have a clear and discernible link to a higher purpose, we, as educators, should attempt to articulate such goals in every one of our courses so as to fulfill our own ambitions for holistic education. As part of their calling, faculty should be encouraged to integrate learning goals and assignments that help students develop in these ways. Liberal arts educators—that is, faculty members, not professional advisors or career center personnel—are best poised to encourage students to think about a higher calling and to guide them as they reflect on their sense of vocation (Lagemann 11). Faculty members must engage students as persons who are searching for more than mastery of the content; they must perform a pastoral role, the role of mentor.

As mentors, faculty members must both encourage and welcome the great questions that give meaning to a student's journey toward independence and maturity. While most assignments will focus on the precise material being explored, occasional assignments that engage students in their relation to the material can aid learning in other respects. Great questions can take at least three forms. *Enduring* questions surface in the eyes of students, such as "What is beauty?" or "What is the meaning of death?" Students also seek out *contemporary* questions, such as "What strategies are most likely to reduce poverty in developing countries?" or "Can religion, which is at the center of so much conflict, also serve as a catalyst for peace?" Finally, students are often captivated by more personal and *existential* ques-tions, such as "What values do I hold higher than all others?" or "What am I looking for in friendship?" These, too, are great questions. Existential questions should be at home in a liberal arts setting that aspires to help students develop as persons. Such questions include: What do I prefer to study? Which questions most intrigue me? What are my greatest talents and passions? How can I best improve? Who are my most appealing and inspiring models? What are my dreams for the future? By what criteria should I identify my most prominent goals? How important for my own sense of identity is recognition from others? What do I think are the greatest moral challenges of my generation, and what will I contribute to addressing them? Where can I make the greatest difference? On what would I be willing to stake my life? Some questions are enduring, contemporary, and existential. A good example would be, Why choose the liberal arts?

To ask such questions with both ambition and honesty is to take an important step toward developing character. Students do not want to be given answers, least of all to their own existential questions, but they do welcome and need encouragement, contexts in which to explore ancillary questions, and categories with which to discover connections between their own questions and larger perspectives on life. Faculty can help students draw connections between the issues of the world and their own motivations by raising questions that link academic inquiry with existential meaning and practical challenges. Students ultimately desire to explore areas that they enjoy and then to channel the skills that they have learned into a life lived with a sense of meaning, a life lived to make a difference. Little makes a greater difference than the encouragement that comes from a mentor who recognizes in a student an emerging capacity or a spark of interest in an important topic.

To realize each of these ambitions for a liberal arts education, most especially the third and most neglected ambition, that of the existential component, we need teachers who by their very lives inspire students. I can recall as an undergraduate wanting to model various developing characteristics on the intellectual and social virtues I recognized among my diverse teachers. One of my teachers who joined us for meals each month in our residential hall had a wonderful capacity to engage us in questions about ourselves, our studies, and our plans but also to ask our views of pressing international questions. He set the bar high. A truly educated person offers grounded opinions and perspectives about such issues and thinks about them often. As young persons develop a sense of themselves, they naturally imitate and reject the behaviors of others, whether it be the kinds of questions they ask, the way they interact with others, the books they read and recommend, or the kinds of meaningful activities they pursue beyond their scholarship and teaching.

Faculty members who teach in the liberal arts are invited to engage students as whole persons, to address broader questions in and out of the classroom, and to serve as role models. Faculty serve in many diverse roles—as models of scholarly engagement, intellectual curiosity, clear thinking, persuasive rhetoric, moral integrity, or community service, to give just a small number of examples. Modeling, even unconscious modeling, can be a much more powerful source of education than explicit discourse. One is reminded of the line attributed to St. Francis: "Preach the Gospel at all times, and if necessary, use words." As James O. Freedman suggests, "By the power of their example, professors engaged in liberal education convey the humane significance of such values as inquiry, integrity, empathy, self-discipline, and craftsmanship" (57–58).

Modeling is a classic idea in pedagogy, recognized already by Plato, who presented Socrates as a model of reason and virtue. Cicero notes that we tend to imitate those we admire and those admired by our community, for good and for ill (*Laws* III.30–33). This pedagogical concept continues in modernity with classical theorists such as Locke and Rousseau. Locke notes that there is "Nothing sinking so gently, and so deep, into Men's Minds, as *Example*" ("Some Thoughts" §82, cf. §§55 and 89). Rousseau writes unambiguously that "man is an imitator" (104, cf. 71, 95, 186). The idea is also prominent among early American thinkers. Thomas Jefferson, for example, writes: "When any original act of charity or of gratitude, for instance, is presented either to our sight or imagination, we are deeply impressed with its beauty and feel a strong desire in ourselves of doing charitable and grateful acts also" (233). While we hope primarily to model good thinking and good action, it does not hurt for students to see our struggles: "Show your weaknesses to your pupil if you want to cure his own. Let him see that you undergo the same struggles which he experiences" (Rousseau 334).

Above all, if faculty members are to inspire students and help them along the path to liberal learning, they must seek to embody the threefold value of a liberal arts education by exhibiting passion and a love for their subject and for the greater questions that surround it; by modeling clear and graceful thinking and asking the difficult questions that challenge us to see a topic more fully; and by living according to a higher calling or mission, both in their passion for scholarship and in their engagement with students, as they seek to develop students' minds and spirits. Teachers model not only ideas. Students attend to the ways in which thoughts influence the way they live. Students have an intuitive sense for the Socratic insight that what is important is not only how to argue for a set of propositions but also how to relate those propositions to how they live and what they value.

The significance of sparking the student's passion for learning is nicely portrayed in a white paper, sponsored by the Teagle Foundation, on economics and liberal education:

> Total classroom contact of students with faculty at college involves less than 1 percent of the students' first 21 years of life, with the major being only about one third of that. This suggests to us that the success or failure of a liberal education, or of the major, depends far more on how the educational process influences a student's passion for learning than it does on the specifics of what they learn in their major. In our view, classroom education is best thought of as a *catalyst for education* as much as it is thought of as *the* education. The implication of this view is that colleges will succeed in providing a liberal education almost independently of what they teach if they *instill a passion for learning in the students*. (Colander and McGoldrick 1–2)

Aspiring learners attend to whether a faculty member sparks their interest in fascinating and meaningful questions, encourages them to aspire to the highest possible standards, and offers a supportive, trusting, and also demanding context for learning (Bain). Faculty who care about student learning will exhibit the courage to grade their students appropriately, and when colleges assess teaching, they should review grading practices as well, so that demanding teachers are not unjustly penalized and easy teachers not unjustly rewarded. A rich evaluation of teaching will ask not only whether students perceive themselves to be well-taught (the so-called student evaluations of teaching) but also whether the faculty member articulates clear learning goals, is current and competent in the field, and develops a well-structured learning environment, and whether the students actually learn. To become a faculty mentor to students is to support them, challenge them, and inspire them.

Such faculty members are able to transcend their specialized research pursuits in such a way as to have a lasting salutary impact on students; indeed, such faculty members change students' lives. Students learn as much from the emulation and appreciation of such persons as they do from the knowledge they possess and the ideas they propose. Here is yet another reason why colleges must continue to cultivate an atmosphere that transcends the dominant categories of the age; the marketplace today does not elevate the intellectual as a model, but if students are to reach their full potential, they will need to encounter intellectuals who live their ideas and who model in this way at least one element of virtue.

A great liberal arts education brings forward not only smart and knowledgeable persons, but also good persons, with a sense of mission. For that reason faculty members have an obligation beyond the conveyance of professional expertise. The university as an institution must transcend the more widely accepted purpose of a college education: academic exploration, critical thinking, and career preparation. It must also nurture a sense of vocation and participatory citizenship, and it must do so across our individual disciplines. Students endeavor not simply to learn a discipline, but to cultivate the mind and the heart. Faculty members who can excel in fostering such learning endeavors, in addition to meeting a college's or university's expectations for scholarship, should be recognized and rewarded in multiple ways. Our greatest challenge is not to help our students find a career that satisfies their specialized intellectual interests and capacities or their material needs and desires but to help them find a higher calling that allows them to gain meaning and to be both at home in the world as it is and active in the wider world as it should be, so that learning becomes service to wisdom and justice. For that, no path is more worthy than a liberal arts education.

Notes

Introduction

1. See *Digest of Education Statistics* table 271. In 1970–71, 50 percent of the majors at American colleges and universities were in the liberal arts. The figure dropped consistently over the next fifteen years, reaching 35 percent in 1985–86. During that same fifteen-year period, business majors grew from 14 percent to 24 percent. Subsequently, liberal arts majors grew modestly; they have leveled out at 40 percent to 42 percent from 1991–92 through 2007–8. For an attempt to explain some of the oscillation over time, with particular attention to gender considerations and enrollment demand (including strategies for attracting and retaining students), see Turner and Bowen.

In 2007–8, the most recent year for which data are available, majors in the liberal arts were divided as follows: social sciences and history (26 percent), psychology (14 percent), visual and performing arts (13 percent), biological and biomedical sciences (12 percent), English (9 percent), liberal arts and sciences, general studies, and humanities (7 percent), multi- and interdisciplinary studies (5 percent), physical sciences (3 percent), foreign languages and literatures (3 percent), mathematics (2 percent), philosophy and religion (2 percent), theology (1 percent), and area, ethnic, cultural, and gender studies (1 percent) (*Digest of Education Statistics* table 271). Because of rounding, the figures deviate slightly from 100 percent.

2. For the older data, see Pryor et al. 72–73; for the most recent data, see "Nation" 18. Although "being very well off financially" ranks as the highest value at 77 percent, close behind in the most recent survey, and higher than in past years, is "helping others who are in difficulty," at 70 percent. Also, "developing a meaningful philosophy of life" is currently on an upward trajectory. In 2003, the figure was at a low point of 39 percent; by 2008, the last year for which we have data, it had risen to 51 percent ("Nation" 18). These trends support my claims concerning the mixed, or complex, goals of today's students, which I explore in chapter 3.

3. The 2006 report of the Commission on the Future of Higher Education was published under the title *A Test of Leadership: Charting the Future of U.S. Higher Education.*

4. Not surprisingly, given the spirit of the age, the *Academic Ranking of World Universities* from Shanghai devotes 0 percent of its ranking to the arts and the humanities, focusing exclusively on awards, publications, and citations in the more practically oriented disciplines of the natural sciences and mathematics; engineering, technology, and computer sciences; life and agriculture sciences; clinical medicine and pharmacy; and the social sciences. Despite the orientation away from the liberal arts, including the humanities, in China and elsewhere, there are rare exceptions, for example, Lingnan University, which describes itself as "The Liberal Arts University in Hong Kong." Among the additional exceptions outside the United States and Western Europe, one might note, for example, Ashesi University in Ghana and Smolny College in Russia. In 2009, three Chinese students who were enrolled as undergraduates at American liberal arts colleges published a book in Chinese on the distinctive aspects of their learning experiences, so as to make China, whose culture has tended to place less emphasis on independence and innovation, aware of this often overlooked option for higher learning in the United States; the book quickly received a second printing (Golden).

5. Wolniak et al. Compare Kuh, Cruce et al., who note that student engagement during the first year in the kind of educationally purposeful practices one finds at liberal arts colleges has had a positive effect on students who entered college with lower levels of academic achievement.

6. I have bracketed engineering, which is on the edge of the liberal arts, and could in principle be integrated. Even though engineering is an applied discipline that transcends learning for its own sake, it does have many of the qualities of the liberal arts. To the extent that engineering and architecture, to take another complex case, can be taught in a liberal arts context—that is, with sufficient courses in the arts, humanities, and social sciences and with an emphasis on the integration of science and mathematics, the conceptual aspects of design and problem solving, and the beauty and history of building as well as the obvious acquisition of broad formal skills and the less than obvious integration of ethical purpose—this integration can elevate both professional and liberal arts curricula. As the world changes, the disciplines change. Hans Jonas has effectively shown the extent to which ethical obligations become different, in quantity and quality, in a world with greater interconnected and distant effects and in a world with global communications. Similarly, what we understand by a liberal arts education could change based on circumstances; a contemporary liberal arts education might well benefit from courses that help to ensure in students a more sophisticated level of technical literacy.

The concept of an integration of engineering and liberal education has been advanced by the National Academy of Engineering in *The Engineer of 2020* and in the proceedings of the annual symposia on engineering and liberal education, which have taken place from 2008 through 2010 at Union College (http://www.union.edu/integration). Still, the challenges in integrating engineering are not trivial. Bok, who expresses concerns about the narrowness of undergraduate engineering majors, writes that it "may well be that success in broadening engineering education will only arrive when engineering becomes a graduate program similar to business and law" (298).

7. On active learning in Rousseau, see, for example, 78, 145, 149, 168, 239, and 255; on learning what is useful or meaningful, see 112, 179, 184–85, and 458.

8. Astin, "Involvement" 124. For additional accounts of the value of active learning, including related issues such as student engagement with faculty and with peers, see, for example, Pascarella and Terenzini 2: 101–2, 122–24, 189–90; Light 45–80; Bransford et al. 121–24; 127–32; Barr and Tagg; Astin, *What Matters* 375–76; 382–87; and Chickering and Gamson. On best practices, which real-

ize active learning and are common in liberal arts settings, see Kuh, *High-Impact Educational Practices*. Astin notes that "residential liberal arts colleges in general, and highly selective liberal arts colleges in particular, produce a pattern of consistently positive student outcomes not found in any other type of American higher-education institution" ("How" 77).

9. Commonly, people speak of the "big questions." Connor could be seen as one example for many. While "big" captures the idea that these are far-reaching questions that transcend individual disciplines, it suggests only a quantitative dimension. I prefer the term "great" questions, which captures their profound and ennobling quality.

10. For the sections on literature, I draw partially on material that is developed further in my book *Why Literature Matters in the 21st Century*.

11. Although I note some reasons why students, faculty, and even society might resist the liberal arts ideal or fail to realize it, my contribution here is not a how-to document on developing such an education. Such an exercise would be mainly of interest to faculty members and administrators, whereas this book is designed to appeal not only to that audience but also to students and parents. Any account of deficiencies must begin with a vision or normative ideal. For a highly engaging discussion of gaps between college as it should be and college as it is, intended primarily for administrators and faculty members, I recommend Bok's *Our Underachieving Colleges*. Schneider and Schoenberg offer a lucid and succinct account of recent advances and current deficiencies in American liberal arts education; it, too, is mainly of interest to faculty members and administrators.

1. *Engaging the Great Questions*

1. On the value of asceticism in Augustine, see, for example, *Confessions* I.20, IX.4, X.28–43, and XIII.22. On contemplation as the highest good in Aristotle, see, for example, *Nicomachean Ethics* X. On Aquinas's view of intellection as what makes us most like God, see, for example, *Summa Theologica* I-II.93.1–9, I-II.3.5, and II-II.182.1–2.

2. Augustine, *On the Trinity* I.17 and Aquinas, *Summa Theologica* I-II.3.4–5. See also Augustine's suggestion that "the only true

state of happiness" is "to rejoice in the truth" (*Confessions* X.23) and Aquinas's argument that "the last and perfect happiness . . . consists entirely in contemplation" (*Summa Theologica* I-II.3.5).

3. See the section "Student and Faculty Expectations" under the "Selected Results" tab of the Faculty Survey of Student Engagement (FSSE) for 2009, online at http://fsse.iub.edu/, which includes data on student reported study time. As an academic discipline, business has been at the bottom in student reported study time since at least 2006.

4. For a condensed version of Gioia's speech, see "The Impoverishment of American Culture."

5. Lessing 13: 23–24: "Not the truth that any person possesses, or imagines she possesses, but the honest effort she makes to discover truth constitutes a person's value. For a person's powers are broadened not in the possession of truth, but rather in the search for truth, and it is in this broadening alone that her ever increasing perfection consists. Possession makes one quiescent, lazy, arrogant."

6. See Oakley, "The Humanities"; Bourque; Cech; and, more recently, Burrelli et al.

7. "The great Thing to be minded in Education is, what *Habits* you settle: And therefore in this, as all other Things, do not begin to make any Thing *customary*, the Practice whereof you would not have continue, and increase" (Locke, "Some Thoughts" §18; cf. §§38, 66, and 200).

2. Cultivating Intellectual and Practical Virtues

1. While we welcome joy for its own sake, as Plato suggests, recent research in evolutionary psychology has suggested that joy also serves a secondary purpose: it broadens our attention, makes us more playful, opens our minds to new possibilities, and gives us energy and resilience for new challenges (Fredrickson, "Role"; Frederickson, "What Good"). While this research modifies Plato's example, it underscores the claim that there are goods, such as a liberal arts education, that are of value both for their own sake and for their aftereffects.

2. On the arts and sciences and critical thinking, see Dressel and Mayhew; see also Forrest 31–34. On the humanities and critical thinking, see Astin, *What Matters* 226–27, 349–50.

3. Emotional intelligence, to which I return below, covers aspects of both intrapersonal and interpersonal intelligence. In *Intelligence Reframed*, Gardner only partially accepts existential intelligence and does not recognize moral intelligence. As a social scientist, Gardner wants only to describe phenomena from a scholarly perspective; he eschews moving beyond the descriptive sphere to "the realm of values" (75). The widespread modern view that value judgments are not scientific and therefore cannot be defended via reason, has not been without its impact, as I note in chapter 3, on the academy's hesitation to engage students in the development of character.

4. See Nussbaum, *Cultivating Humanity* 50–84 and, more recently, *Not for Profit* 79–94. *Not for Profit*, which appeared after my manuscript had gone through the copyediting stage, makes a case for the utility of the liberal arts not for economic purposes but for political purposes, arguing that critical thinking and empathy are crucial for democracy and human development.

5. On helping students learn by setting high expectations, see Bain 68–97; Chickering and Gamson; and Sorcinelli 20–21.

6. Useem, "What" 71; cf. Useem, *Liberal Education* 91–102.

7. On the economic advantages to those who graduate from liberal arts colleges and universities, especially selective private institutions, see Getz 33–38; Dey and Hill 28; Pascarella and Terenzini 2: 469–76; Brewer et al.; Bowen and Bok 118–54; Eide et al.; Eide and Waehrer; and Useem, *Liberal Education*. Useem, for example, notes the role of cultural norms and preferences within firms (128). One of the complex puzzles debated in the literature is the extent to which the already strong academic abilities of the students or their distinctive college experiences are more significant factors in determining their earnings.

8. On the value of liberal arts education for developing countries and recommendations for its implementation, see Bloom and Rosovsky.

9. One could argue that the two most common practical pitfalls of otherwise successful liberal arts graduates are, on the one hand, not exhibiting in their course selection enough attention to classes that develop quantitative thinking and ensure a facility with numbers (studies consistently show that the one area in which liberal arts students, especially humanities majors, perform below the level of business and engineering majors is in quantitative skills)

and, on the other hand, not being sufficiently proactive in seeking out opportunities, by way of the campus career center and other avenues, to help ease the transition from exploring the liberal arts to identifying a meaningful vocation. The latter can derive from many factors, including a false lack of confidence about their fit for a career in business.

The link between the intrinsic value of learning and the transition to a career needs more focus on most American campuses. Of eleven categories evaluated in the 2005 College Student Survey, graduating students ranked "job placement services for students" by far the lowest; only 45 percent of students were "satisfied" or "very satisfied" with those services. Also ranking relatively low was "career counseling and advising," at 54 percent (Saenz and Barrera 5). One of the main arguments of this chapter has been that a focus on learning for its own sake and a focus on learning for a career are not at all incompatible goods, but either many colleges are unable to develop equal levels of excellence in both areas or many students fail to take advantage of both opportunities.

3. *Forming Character*

1. Since at least 2006, "thinking critically and analytically" is the most highly elevated category. The next highest, "learning effectively on their own," is related insofar as it points toward independence of thought. To think critically is to be able to think for oneself. The data are available under "Course-Based Option," "Total Grand Frequency" in the FSSE reports from 2003 to 2009, available online at http://fsse.iub.edu. For the 2009 survey, see *FSSE 2009 Total Grand Frequencies* 21–23.

2. Lindholm et al. 40. The percentage of faculty interested in value questions rose dramatically from 2004–5 to 2007–8. The comparisons are as follows: "enhance students' self-understanding," up from 60 percent to 72 percent; "develop moral character," up from 59 percent to 70 percent; and "help students develop personal values," up from 53 percent to 66 percent (Lindholm et al. 40; DeAngelo et al. 35). The trend, if it should continue, would weaken claims about the level of current obstacles to be overcome and strengthen confidence about the possibility that the third purpose of a liberal arts education can still be realized today.

3. *FSSE 2009 Frequency Distributions, Baccalaureate Colleges* 21–23. The 2009 figures are promising in relation to the 2008 figures. In 2008, the figures were 42 percent (versus 50 percent in 2009) for "quite a bit" or "very much" emphasis on helping students develop "a personal code of values and ethics"; and 47 percent (versus 57 percent in 2009) for emphasis on students "understanding themselves" (*FSSE 2008* 23, 22).

4. A partial exception arises at selective liberal arts colleges, where a relatively high percentage of faculty members believe that moral values and self-knowledge are very important undergraduate goals (Ruscio 216–17).

5. The classic statement of the separation of knowledge and morality is Max Weber's essay "Science as a Vocation." Reuben offers an illuminating account of historical transitions in American higher education, which were increasingly directed toward this separation.

6. The claim that religion is private and ultimately beyond reason is a modern view, which is widely shared by contemporary educators (see, for example, Light 162–63; and Kronman *Education's End* 198–99) but is contested by prominent medieval representatives of all three great monotheistic traditions as well as by modern thinkers who sought to interpret religion in the light of reason, such as Hegel, or who argue for the harmony of faith and reason, such as John Paul II. For the relevance of this tradition for the idea of a university, see Roche, *The Intellectual Appeal.*

7. On diversity as aiding learning, see Page; Pascarella and Terenzini 2: 130–32, 193–94; Gurin et al.; and Light 40–44, 47–50, 129–89.

8. Nie and Hillygus 45. Compare Astin, *What Matters* 370, who notes that majoring in business has a negative effect on altruism, social activism, and commitment to promoting racial understanding.

9. On the value of tying experiences inside the classroom to student concerns outside the classroom, see Pascarella and Terenzini 2: 128–30, 194–96; and Light 113–18, 87–91, 110–13.

10. For the rationale and description of the World Masterpieces Seminar, I draw on Fallon and Power. One of the inspirations for the seminar was the Clemente project, which involved teaching great works in the humanities to economically disadvantaged adults in New York City. For a description of that project, see Shorris 353–85, 402–8.

11. The phrase "preferential option for the poor," while drawing on sources as ancient as the Old Testament embrace of the widow, the orphan, and the poor and as recent as the Second Vatican Council, derives from the conferences of the Latin American Bishops that took place in Medellín, Colombia, in 1968 and in Puebla, Mexico, in 1979. The term was later adopted by the United States Conference of Catholic Bishops, where it was used extensively, for example, in their 1986 document *Economic Justice For All: Pastoral Letter on Catholic Social Teaching and the U.S. Economy,* and by John Paul II in his 1987 encyclical *On Social Concern.*

12. The descriptions of the participants and the quotations stem directly from Bronner.

Works Cited

Academic Ranking of World Universities. Shanghai: ShanghaiRanking Consultancy, 2009. Available at http://www.arwu.org/ (last accessed April 2010).

Apel, Karl-Otto. *Transformation der Philosophie.* 6th ed. Frankfurt: Suhrkamp, 2002.

Aquinas, Saint Thomas. *Summa Theologica.* Trans. Fathers of the English Dominican Province. 2nd ed. 5 vols. Westminster, Maryland: Christian Classics, 1981.

Astin, Alexander W. "How the Liberal Arts College Affects Students." *Daedalus* 128.1 (1999): 77–100.

————. "Involvement in Learning Revisited: Lessons We Have Learned." *Journal of College Student Development* 37.2 (1996): 123–33.

————. *What Matters in College? Four Critical Years Revisited.* San Francisco: Jossey-Bass, 1993.

Augustine, Saint. *The City of God.* Trans. Marcus Dods, D.D. New York: Random House, 1950.

————. *Confessions.* Trans. R. S. Pine-Coffin. New York: Penguin, 1961.

Bain, Ken. *What the Best College Teachers Do.* Cambridge: Harvard University Press, 2004.

Baldwin, Roger G., and Vicki L. Baker. "The Case of the Disappearing Liberal Arts College." *Inside Higher Ed* 9 July 2009. Available at http://www.insidehighered.com/views/2009/07/09/baldwin (last accessed April 2010).

Barker, Carol M. *Liberal Arts Education for a Global Society.* New York: Carnegie Corporation of New York, 2000. Available at http://carnegie.org/fileadmin/Media/Publications/PDF/libarts. pdf (last accessed April 2010).

Barr, Robert B., and John Tagg. "From Teaching to Learning: A New Paradigm for Undergraduate Education." *Change* 27.6 (1995): 13–25.

Barzun, Jacques. *The House of Intellect.* New York: Harper, 1959.

Beck, Robert E. *Career Patterns: The Liberal Arts Major in Bell System Management.* Washington, DC: Association of American Colleges, 1981.

Benoliel, Peter A. "Liberal Education: Preparing Tomorrow's Business Executives." *Higher Education, Human Resources, and the National Economy.* Washington, DC: Association of American Colleges, 1974. 117–23.

Bernstein, Theodore M. *The Careful Writer: A Modern Guide to English Usage.* New York: Atheneum, 1984.

Bisconti, Ann Stoufer, and Jean G. Kessler. *College and Other Stepping Stones: A Study of Learning Experiences that Contribute to Effective Performance in Early and Long-run Jobs.* Bethlehem, PA: College Placement Council Foundation, 1980.

Blanshard, Brand. *The Uses of a Liberal Education, and Other Talks to Students.* LaSalle, IL: Open Court, 1973.

Bloom, Allan. *The Closing of the American Mind: How Higher Education Has Failed Democracy and Impoverished the Souls of America's Students.* New York: Simon and Schuster, 1987.

Bloom, David E., and Henry Rosovsky. "Liberal Education: Why Developing Countries Should Not Neglect It." *Liberal Education* 89.1 (2003): 16–23.

Bogle, John C. *Enough: True Measures of Money, Business, and Life.* Hoboken, NJ: Wiley & Sons, 2009.

Bok, Derek. *Our Underachieving Colleges: A Candid Look at How Much Students Learn and Why They Should be Learning More.* Princeton: Princeton University Press, 2006.

Bosanquet, Bernard. *Collected Works of Bernard Bosanquet.* Ed. William Sweet. 20 vols. Bristol: Thoemmes Press, 1999.

Botstein, Leon. "The Curriculum and College Life: Confronting Unfilled Promises." *Declining by Degrees: Higher Education at Risk.*

Ed. Richard H. Hersh and John Merrow. New York: Macmillan, 2005. 209–28.

Bourque, Susan C. "Reassessing Research: Liberal Arts Colleges and the Social Sciences." *Daedalus* 128.1 (1999): 265–72.

Bowen, William G., and Derek Bok. *The Shape of the River: Long-term Consequences of Considering Race in College and University Admissions.* Princeton: Princeton University Press, 1998.

Boyer, Ernest L. *College: The Undergraduate Experience in America.* New York: Harper & Row, 1987.

Branham, Leigh. *The 7 Hidden Reasons Employees Leave: How to Recognize the Subtle Signs and Act before It's Too Late.* New York: American Management Association, 2005.

Bransford, John D., Ann L. Brown, and Rodney R. Cocking, eds. *How People Learn: Brain, Mind, Experience, and School.* Washington, DC: National Academy Press, 1999.

Breneman, David W. "Are We Losing Our Liberal Arts Colleges?" *AAHE Bulletin* 43.2 (October 1990): 3–6.

Brewer, Dominic J., Eric R. Eide, and Ronald G. Ehrenberg. "Does It Pay to Attend an Elite Private College? Cross-Cohort Evidence on the Effects of College Type on Earnings." *Journal of Human Resources* 34.1 (1999): 104–23.

Brint, Steven, Mark Riddle, Lori Turk-Bicakci, and Charles S. Levy. "From the Liberal to the Practical Arts in American Colleges and Universities: Organizational Analysis and Curricular Change." *Journal of Higher Education* 76.2 (2005): 151–80.

Broch, Hermann. *The Sleepwalkers.* Trans. Willa and Edwin Muir. San Francisco: North Point, 1985.

Bronner, Ethan. "For the Homeless, Rebirth through Socrates." *New York Times* 7 March 1999. Available at http://www.nytimes.com/ 1999/03/07/us/for-the-homeless-rebirth-through-socrates .html?pagewanted=1 (last accessed April 2010).

Brooks, David. "The Organization Kid." *Atlantic Monthly* 287 (4 April 2001): 40–54.

Burrelli, Joan, Alan Rapoport, and Rolf Lehming. "Baccalaureate Origins of S&E Doctorate Recipients." *InfoBrief SRS. Science Resource Statistics.* National Science Foundation, NSF 08311, July 2008. Available at http://www.nsf.gov/statistics/infbrief/ nsf08311/nsf08311.pdf (last accessed April 2010).

Burtchaell, James Turnstead, C.S.C. "Major Decisions: How to Pick Your Major in College." *Notre Dame Magazine* 15.4 (1986–87): 24–27.

Calvert, Robert, Jr. *Career Patterns of Liberal Arts Graduates.* 2nd ed. Cranston, RI: Carroll Press, 1973.

Cech, Thomas R. "Science at Liberal Arts Colleges: A Better Education?" *Daedelus* 128.1 (1999): 195–216.

Chace, William M. *100 Semesters: My Adventures as Student, Professor, and University President, and What I Learned Along the Way.* Princeton: Princeton University Press, 2006.

Chekhov, Anton. "The Student." *Anton Chekhov's Short Stories.* Ed. Ralph E. Matlaw. New York: Norton, 1979. 106–9.

Chickering, Arthur W., and Zelda F. Gamson, eds. *Applying the Seven Principles for Good Practice in Undergraduate Education.* San Francisco: Jossey-Bass, 1991.

Colander, David, and KimMarie McGoldrick. *The Economics Major and a Liberal Education. Draft Teagle Foundation Report.* New York: Teagle Foundation, 2008. Available at http://www.teagle foundation.org/learning/pdf/2008_aea_whitepaper.pdf (last accessed April 2010).

Colby, Anne, Thomas Ehrlich, Elizabeth Beaumont, and Jason Stephens. *Educating Citizens: Preparing America's Undergraduates for Lives of Moral and Civic Responsibility.* San Francisco: Jossey-Bass, 2003.

College Learning for the New Global Century: A Report from the National Leadership Council for Liberal Education and America's Promise. Washington, DC: Association of American Colleges and Universities, 2007.

Collins, Randall. *The Sociology of Philosophies: A Global Theory of Intellectual Change.* Cambridge: Harvard University Press, 1998.

Connor, W. Robert. "Watching Charlotte Climb: Little Steps toward Big Questions." *Liberal Education* 93.2 (2007): 6–13.

Cook, Claire. *Line by Line: How to Edit Your Own Writing.* New York: Modern Language Association, 1985.

Cronon, William. "'Only Connect': The Goals of a Liberal Arts Education." *Liberal Education* 85.1 (1999): 6–12.

Damon, William. *The Path to Purpose: Helping Our Children Find Their Calling in Life.* New York: Free Press, 2008.

DeAngelo, Linda, Sylvia Hurtado, John H. Pryor, Kimberly R. Kelly, José Luis Santos, and William S. Korn. *The American College Teacher: National Norms for the 2007–2008 HERI Faculty Survey.* Los Angeles: Higher Education Research Institute, UCLA, 2009.

Delbanco, Andrew. "The Endangered University." *New York Review of Books* 52.5 (24 March 2005). Available at http://www.ny books.com/articles/17856 (last accessed July 2009).

Dewey, John. *Democracy and Education: An Introduction to the Philosophy of Education.* 1916. New York: Free Press, 1944.

Dey, Judy Goldberg, and Catherine Hill. *Behind the Pay Gap.* Washington, DC: Association of American University Women Educational Foundation, 2007.

Digest of Education Statistics: 2009. Washington, DC: National Center for Education Statistics, n.d. Available at http://nces.ed.gov/ programs/digest/d09/ (last accessed April 2010).

Drahos, Kristen. [Notre Dame Bachelor of Arts graduate in theology and philosophy, 2009]. Undated letter to author.

Dressel, Paul L. and Lewis B. Mayhew. *General Education: Explorations in Evaluation: The Final Report of the Cooperative Study of the Evaluation in General Education of the American Council on Education.* Washington, DC: American Council on Education, 1954.

Eide, Eric, Dominic J. Brewer, and Ronald G. Ehrenberg. "Does It Pay to Attend an Elite Private College? Evidence on the Effects of Undergraduate College Quality on Graduate School Attendance." *Economics of Education Review* 17.4 (1998): 371–76.

Eide, Eric, and Geetha Waehrer. "The Role of the Option Value of College Attendance in College Major Choice." *Economics of Education Review* 17.2 (1998): 73–82.

The Engineer of 2020: Visions of Engineering in the New Century. By National Academy of Engineering. Washington, DC: National Academies Press, 2004.

Executive Summary. Survey of Indiana Employers: Liberal Arts Skills and Attitudes. Indianapolis: Independent Colleges of Indiana, 2003.

Fallon, Stephen, and F. Clark Power. "World Masterpieces Seminar." Program of Liberal Studies. University of Notre Dame, Notre Dame, IN. Available at http://pls.nd.edu/about/com munity-extensions/documents/CommunityExtension.pdf (last accessed April 2010).

Fischer, Karen. "Professors Get Their Own Study-Abroad Programs: Trips for Faculty Members Are Promoted to Raise Students' Global Awareness." *Chronicle of Higher Education* 31 October 2008: A1.

Fish, Stanley. "Aim Low: Confusing Democratic Values with Academic Ones Can Easily Damage the Quality of Education." *Chronicle of Higher Education* 16 May 2003: C5.

———. *Save the World on Your Own Time.* New York: Oxford University Press, 2008.

———. "Why We Built the Ivory Tower." *New York Times* 21 May 2004. Available at http://www.nytimes.com/2004/05/21/opinion/why-we-built-the-ivory-tower.html (last accessed April 2010).

Follett, Wilson. *Modern American Usage: A Guide.* Ed. Jacques Barzun. New York: Hill & Wang, 1966.

Forrest, Aubrey. *Increasing Student Competence and Persistence: The Best Case for General Education.* Iowa City: American College Testing Program, 1982.

Franke, Richard J. "The Power of the Humanities and a Challenge to Humanists." *Daedalus* 138.1 (2009): 13–23.

Frankfurter, Felix. *Of Law and Men: Papers and Addresses of Felix Frankfurter, 1939–1956.* Ed. Philip Elman. New York: Harcourt Brace, 1956.

Franklin, Benjamin. "Proposals Relating to the Education of Youth in Pennsylvania." *The Autobiography and Other Writings on Politics, Economics, and Virtue.* Ed. Alan Houston. Cambridge: Cambridge University Press, 2004. 203–14.

Fredrickson, Barbara L. "The Role of Positive Emotions in Positive Psychology: The Broaden-and-Build Theory of Positive Emotions." *American Psychologist* 56 (2001): 218–26.

———. "What Good are Positive Emotions?" *Review of General Psychology* 2 (1998): 300–319.

Freedman, James O. *Idealism and Liberal Education.* Ann Arbor: University of Michigan Press, 1996.

Friedman, Thomas L. *The World is Flat: A Brief History of the Twenty-first Century.* New York: Farrar, Straus and Giroux, 2005.

FSSE 2008 Frequency Distributions, Baccalaureate Colleges Arts & Sciences. Bloomington, IN: National Survey of Student Engagement, 2008. Available at http://nsse.iub.edu/pdf/2008_Institutional_Report/FSSE08%20Reports%20(Bac-A&S%20-%20CB).pdf (last accessed April 2010).

FSSE 2009 Frequency Distributions, Baccalaureate Colleges Arts & Sciences. Bloomington, IN: National Survey of Student

Engagement, 2009. Available at http://fsse.iub.edu/pdf/FSSE_IR
_2009/FSSE09%20Reports%20(Bac-A&S).pdf (last accessed
April 2010).

FSSE 2009 Frequency Distributions, Total Grand Frequencies. Bloom-
ington, IN: National Survey of Student Engagement, 2009.
Available at http://fsse.iub.edu/pdf/FSSE_IR_2009/FSSE09%20
Reports%20(Total-CB).pdf (last accessed April 2010).

Gardner, Howard. *Frames of Mind: The Theory of Multiple Intelligences.* New York: Basic Books, 1985.

———. *Intelligence Reframed: Multiple Intelligences for the 21st
Century.* New York: Basic Books, 1999.

Gehlen, Arnold. *Man in the Age of Technology.* Trans. Patricia Lip-
scomb. New York: Columbia University Press, 1980.

Getz, Malcolm. *Investing in College: A Guide for the Perplexed.* Cambridge: Harvard University Press, 2007.

Gioia, Dana. "The Impoverishment of American Culture."
Wall Street Journal 19 July 2007. Available at http://www
.opinionjournal.com/la/?id=110010352 (last accessed December 2009).

Glenn, David. "2 Colleges in Vermont, 2 Paths that Defy Tradition."
Chronicle of Higher Education 5 March 2010: A22–24.

Goethe, Johann Wolfgang von. *Faust.* Ed. Erich Trunz. Munich: Beck,
1972.

Golden, Serena. "'A True Liberal Arts Education.'" *Inside Higher Ed.*
Available at http://www.insidehighered.com/news/2009/10/16/
liberalarts (last accessed April 2010).

Goleman, Daniel. *Emotional Intelligence: Why It Can Matter More
Than IQ.* New York: Bantam Books, 2005.

Goleman, Daniel, Richard Boyatzis, and Annie McKee. *Primal Leadership: Realizing the Power of Emotional Intelligence.* Boston:
Harvard Business School Press, 2002.

Gouldner, Alvin W. "Cosmopolitans and Locals: Toward an Analysis of Latent Social Roles, I and II." *Administrative Science
Quarterly* 2 (December 1957 and March 1958): 281–306 and
444–80.

Goyette, Kimberly A., and Ann L. Mullen. "Who Studies the Arts and
Sciences? Social Background and the Choice and Consequences
of Undergraduate Field of Study." *Journal of Higher Education*
77 (2006): 497–538.

Graber, Robert Bates. *Valuing Useless Knowledge.* Kirksville, Mis-
souri: Thomas Jefferson University Press, 1995.

Greater Expectations: A New Vision for Learning as a Nation Goes to College. A National Panel Report. Washington, DC: Association of American Colleges and Universities, 2002.

Guren, Adam M., and Natalie I. Sherman, "Harvard Graduates Head to Investment Banking, Consulting: Results from the Class of 2008 Survey." *Harvard Crimson* 22 June 2008. Available at http://www.thecrimson.com/printerfriendly.aspx?ref=523900 (last accessed April 2010).

Gurin, Patricia, Eric L. Dey, Sylvia Hurtado, and Gerald Gurin. "Diversity and Higher Education: Theory and Impact on Educational Outcomes." *Harvard Education Review* 72 (2002): 330–66.

Habermas, Jürgen. *Theorie des kommunikativen Handelns.* 6th ed. 2 vols. Frankfurt: Suhrkamp, 2006.

Harper, Stephen C. "Business Education: A View from the Top." *Business Forum* (Spring 1987): 24–27.

Harpham, Geoffrey Galt. "The Humanities' Value." *Chronicle of Higher Education* 20 March 2009: B6.

Harris, W. T. "Commentary and Analysis." In *The Philosophy of Education.* By Johann Karl Friedrich Rosenkranz. 2nd ed. New York: Appleton & Co., 1889.

Heath, Douglas H. "What the Enduring Effects of Higher Education Tell Us about a Liberal Education." *Journal of Higher Education* 47 (1976): 173–90.

Hegel, G. W. F. *Werke in zwanzig Bänden.* Ed. Eva Moldenhauer and Karl Markus Michel. Frankfurt: Suhrkamp, 1978.

Hersh, Richard H. "Intentions and Perceptions: A National Survey of Public Attitudes toward Liberal Arts Education." *Change* 29.2 (1997): 16–23.

———. "The Liberal Arts College: The Most Practical and Professional Education for the Twenty-first Century." *Liberal Education* 83.3 (Summer 1997): 26–33.

Hofstadter, Richard. *Anti-intellectualism in American Life.* New York: Knopf, 1963.

Hollinger, David A. *Cosmopolitanism and Solidarity: Studies in Ethnoracial, Religious, and Professional Affiliation in the United States.* Madison: University of Wisconsin Press, 2006.

Holmes, Oliver Wendell, Jr. *The Essential Holmes.* Ed. Richard A. Posner. Chicago: University of Chicago Press, 1992.

Hösle, Vittorio. "Crises of Identity: Individual and Collective." *Objective Idealism, Ethics, and Politics.* Notre Dame, IN: University of Notre Dame Press, 1998. 83–100.

———. "'Great Books Programs.' Die Rolle der Klassiker im Bildungsprozeß." *Kultur, Bildung oder Geist? Skizzen zur Gestalt der europäischen Humanwisssenschaften im 21. Jahrhundert.* Ed. Roland Benedikter. Innsbruck: Studien Verlag, 2004. 117–33.

———. *Die Krise der Gegenwart und die Verantwortung der Philosophie: Transzendentalpragmatik, Letztbegründung, Ethik.* 3rd ed. Munich: Beck, 1997.

———. *Morals and Politics.* Trans. Steven Rendall. Notre Dame, IN: University of Notre Dame Press, 2004.

———. *Der philosophische Dialog.* Munich: Beck, 2006.

Howard, Ann. "College Experiences and Managerial Performance." *Journal of Applied Psychology* 71 (1986): 530–52.

"How Should Colleges Assess and Improve Student Learning? Employers' Views on the Accountability Challenge." Washington, DC: Peter. D. Hart Research Associates, 2008. Available at http://www.aacu.org/LEAP/documents/2008_Business_Leader _Poll.pdf (last accessed April 2010).

Huizinga, Johan. *Homo Ludens: A Study of the Play-Element in Culture.* Boston: Beacon, 1950.

Humboldt, Wilhelm von. *Werke in fünf Bänden.* Ed. Andreas Flitner and Klaus Giel. Darmstadt: Wissenschaftliche Buchgesellschaft, 1964.

Hurtado, Sylvia, Linda J. Sax, Victor Saenz, Casandra E. Harper, Leticia Oseguera, Jennifer Curley, Lina Lopez, De'Sha Wolf, and Lucy Arellano. *Findings from the 2005 Administration of Your First College Year (YFCY): National Aggregates.* Los Angeles: Higher Education Research Institute, UCLA, 2007.

Hutchins, Robert M. "President Hutchins's First Convocation Address." *University of Chicago Record,* n.s. 15 (1929): 119–23.

Jaspers, Karl. *Die Idee der Universität.* 1946. Berlin: Springer, 1980.

Jean Paul. *Jean Pauls Werke in vier Bänden.* Munich: Langen, 1925.

Jefferson, Thomas. *Political Writings.* Ed. Joyce Appleby and Terrence Ball. Cambridge: Cambridge University Press, 1999.

Job Outlook 2010. Bethlehem, PA: National Association of Colleges and Employers, 2009.

John Paul II. *Fides et Ratio. On the Relationship between Faith and Reason.* Boston: Pauline, 1998.

Jonas, Hans. *The Imperative of Responsibility. In Search of an Ethics for the Technological Age.* Trans. Hans Jonas with the collaboration of David Herr. Chicago: University of Chicago Press, 1984.

Kant, Immanuel. *Werkausgabe*. Ed. Wilhelm Weischedel. 12 vols. Frankfurt: Suhrkamp, 1968.

Kasser, Tim. *The High Price of Materialism*. Cambridge: MIT Press, 2002.

Katchadourian, Herant and John Boli. *Cream of the Crop: The Impact of Elite Education in the Decade after College*. New York: Basic-Books, 1994.

Kauffmann, Norman L., Judith N. Martin, and Henry D. Weaver. *Students Abroad: Strangers at Home. Education for a Global Society*. Yarmouth, ME: Intercultural Press, 1992.

Kearns, David T. Foreword. *Reclaiming the Legacy: In Defense of Liberal Education*. By Denis P. Doyle. Washington, DC: Council for Basic Education, 2000. Available at http://web.archive.org/web/20010108184200/www.c-b-e.org/pubs/doylebk.htm (last accessed April 2009).

Keup, Jennifer R., and Ellen Bara Stolzenberg. *The 2003 Your First College Year (YFCY) Survey: Exploring the Academic and Personal Experiences of First-Year Students*. Columbia, South Carolina: National Resource Center for the First-Year Experience and Students in Transition, 2004.

Kimball, Bruce A. *Orators and Philosophers: A History of the Idea of Liberal Education*. New York: Teachers College Press, 1986.

Kleist, Heinrich von. "Über die allmähliche Verfertigung der Gedanken beim Reden." *Schriften*. 6th ed. Munich: Hanser, 1977. 2: 319–324.

Kliff, Sarah. "Well-Rounded Docs: That's the Goal as Medical Schools Seek Out and Admit More Nonscience Students. English Majors Welcome." *Newsweek* 10 September 2007. Available at http://www.newsweek.com/id/40747 (last accessed April 2010).

Knox, William E., Paul Lindsay, and Mary N. Kolb. *Does College Make a Difference? Long-term Changes in Activities and Attitudes*. Westport, CT: Greenwood Press, 1993.

Kristeller, Paul Oskar. "The Modern System of the Arts: A Study in the History of Aesthetics." *Journal of the History of Ideas* 12 (1951): 496–527 and 13 (1952): 17–46.

Kronman, Anthony T. *Education's End: Why Our Colleges and Universities Have Given Up on the Meaning of Life*. New Haven: Yale University Press, 2007.

————. *The Lost Lawyer: Failing Ideals of the Legal Profession*. Cambridge: Harvard University Press, 1993.

Kuh, George D. "Built to Engage: Liberal Arts Colleges and Effective Educational Practice." *Liberal Arts Colleges in American Higher Education: Challenges and Opportunities.* ACLS Occasional Paper 59. New York: American Council of Learned Societies, 2005. 122–50.

———. *High-Impact Educational Practices: What They Are, Who Has Access to Them, and Why They Matter.* Washington, DC: Association of American Colleges and Universities, 2008.

———. "How Are We Doing? Tracking the Quality of the Undergraduate Experience, 1960s to the Present." *Review of Higher Education* 22 (1999): 99–120.

Kuh, George D., Ty M. Cruce, Rick Shoup, Jillian Kinzie, and Robert M. Gonyea. "Unmasking the Effects of Student Engagement on First-Year College Grades and Persistence." *Journal of Higher Education* 79 (2008): 540–63.

Kuh, George D., Jillian Kinzie, John H. Schuh, Elizabeth J. Whitt, and Associates. *Student Success in College: Creating Conditions that Matter.* San Francisco: Jossey-Bass, 2005.

Lagemann, Ellen Condliffe. "The Challenge of Liberal Education: Past, Present, and Future." *Liberal Education* 89.2 (2003): 6–13.

Layard, Richard. *Happiness: Lessons from a New Science.* New York: Penguin, 2005.

Lessing, Gotthold Ephraim. *Gotthold Ephraim Lessings sämtliche Schriften.* 23 vols. Ed. Karl Lachmann. 3rd ed. Stuttgart: Göschen, 1886–1924.

Levin, Richard C. *The Work of the University.* New Haven: Yale University Press, 2003.

Lewis, Harry R. *Excellence without a Soul: How a Great University Forgot Education.* New York: PublicAffairs, 2006.

Lewis, Stephen R., Jr. "The Liberal Arts College: America's Unique Contribution to Higher Education and the Case for its Intrinsic Value." *The Liberal Arts: Lingnan University and the World.* Ed. Eugene Eoyang. Hong Kong: Lingnang University, 2002. 123–49.

Light, Richard J. *Making the Most of College: Students Speak Their Minds.* Cambridge: Harvard University Press, 2001.

Lindholm, Jennifer A., and Katalin Szelényi, Sylvia Hurtado, and William S. Korn. *The American College Teacher: National Norms for the 2004–2005 HERI Faculty Survey.* Los Angeles: Higher Education Research Institute, UCLA, 2005.

Livingston, Rick. "The Humanities for Cocktail Parties—and Beyond." *Chronicle of Higher Education* 7 January 2005: B 5.

Locke, John. *Of the Conduct of the Understanding*. Ed. Ruth W. Grant and Nathan Tarcov. Indianapolis: Hackett, 1996.

―――. "Some Thoughts concerning Education." *The Educational Writings of John Locke*. Ed. James L. Axtell. Cambridge: Cambridge University Press, 1968.114–325.

"McKinsey Global Survey of Business Executives, March 2004." *McKinsey Quarterly*. Available at http://www.mckinseyquarterly .com/Operations/outsourcing/The_McKinsey_Global_Survey _of_Business_Executives__March_2004_1411 (last accessed April 2010).

McLean, Bethany. "Is Enron Overpriced?" *Fortune* 5 March 2001. Available at http://money.cnn.com/2006/01/13/news/ companies/enronoriginal_fortune/index.htm (last accessed April 2010).

McNeel, Steven P. "College Teaching and Student Moral Development." *Moral Development in the Professions: Psychology and Applied Ethics*. Ed. James R. Rest and Darcia Narváez. Hillsdale, NJ: L. Erlbaum, 1994. 27–49.

McPherson, Michael S. "The Economic Value of a Liberal Arts Education." *About Campus* (September–October 1998): 13–17.

Mearsheimer, John J. "The Aims of Education." Philosophy and Literature 22.1 (1998) 133–55. Available at http://muse.jhu.edu/ journals/philosophy_and_literature/v022/22.1mearsheimer01 .html (last accessed April 2010).

Medical School Admission Requirements, United States and Canada, 2002–2003. Washington, DC: Association of American Medical Colleges, 2001.

Medical School Admission Requirements, United States and Canada, 2008–2009. Washington, DC: Association of American Medical Colleges, 2007.

Moevs, Christian. Sheedy Award Address. University of Notre Dame, Notre Dame, IN. 7 September 2006. Available at http://al.nd .edu/assets/16916/2006_sheedyaward_christianmoevs.pdf (last accessed April 2010).

Montaigne, Michel de. *The Complete Essays*. Trans. M. A. Screech. New York: Penguin, 2003.

"The Nation Students: Views." *Chronicle of Higher Education: Almanac Issue 2009–10* 28 August 2009: 18.

Newman, John Henry Cardinal. *The Idea of a University Defined and Illustrated in Nine Discourses Delivered to the Catholics of Dublin in Occasional Lectures and Essays Addressed to Members of the Catholic University.* Ed. Martin J. Svaglic. Notre Dame, IN: University of Notre Dame Press, 1982.

Nie, Norman, and D. Sunshine Hillygus. "Education and Democratic Citizenship." *Making Good Citizens: Education and Civil Society.* Ed. Diane Ravitch and Joseph Viteritti. New Haven. Yale University Press, 2001. 30–57.

Nussbaum, Martha C. *Cultivating Humanity: A Classical Defense of Reform in Liberal Education.* Cambridge: Harvard University Press, 1997.

———. *Love's Knowledge: Essays on Philosophy and Literature.* New York: Oxford University Press, 1990.

———. *Not for Profit: Why Democracy Needs the Humanities.* Princeton: Princeton University Press, 2010.

Oakley, Francis. *Community of Learning: The American College and the Liberal Arts Tradition.* Oxford: Oxford University Press, 1992.

———. "The Humanities in Liberal Arts Colleges: Another Instance of Collegiate Exceptionalism?" *Daedalus* 128.1 (1999): 35–51.

Open Doors: 2008 Report on International Educational Exchange. New York: Institute of International Education, 2008. Available at http://opendoors.iienetwork.org/ (last accessed December 2008).

Orange, Linwood E. *English: The Preprofessional Major.* 4th ed. New York: Modern Language Association, 1986.

Page, Scott E. *The Difference: How the Power of Diversity Creates Better Groups, Firms, Schools, and Societies.* Princeton: Princeton University Press, 2007.

Pascal, Blaise. *Pensées.* Ed. Philippe Sellier. Paris: Garnier, 1991.

Pascarella, Ernest T. and Patrick T. Terenzini. *How College Affects Students.* Vol. 1, *Findings and Insights from Twenty Years of Research.* San Francisco: Jossey-Bass, 1991.

———. *How College Affects Students.* Vol. 2, *A Third Decade of Research.* San Francisco: Jossey-Bass, 2005.

Pascarella, Ernest T., Gregory C. Wolniak, Tricia A. D. Seifert, Ty M. Cruce, and Charles F. Blaich. *Liberal Arts Colleges and Liberal Arts Education: New Evidence on Impacts.* San Francisco: Jossey-Bass, 2005.

Paul Klee: Catalogue Raisonné. Ed. Paul Klee Foundation. Museum of Fine Arts, Berne. 9 vols. New York: Thames and Hudson, 1988–2004.

Pieper, Joseph. *Leisure: The Basis of Culture.* Trans. Gerald Malsbary. South Bend, IN: St. Augustine's Press, 1998.

Plato. *The Collected Dialogues including the Letters.* Ed. Edith Hamilton and Huntington Cairns. Princeton: Princeton University Press, 1978.

Postman, Neil. *Amusing Ourselves to Death: Public Discourse in the Age of Show Business.* 1985. New York: Penguin, 1986.

Pryor, John H, and Sylvia Hurtado, Victor B. Saenz, José Luis Santos, and William S. Korn. *The American Freshman: Forty Year Trends.* Los Angeles: Higher Education Research Institute, UCLA, 2007.

Putnam, Robert. "*E Pluribus Unum*: Diversity and Community in the Twenty-first Century. The 2006 Johan Skytte Prize Lecture." *Scandinavian Political Studies* 30 (2007): 137–74.

Reading at Risk: A Survey of Literary Reading in America. Research Division Report #46. Washington, DC: National Endowment for the Arts, 2004.

Report of the Task Force on General Education. Harvard University Faculty of Arts and Sciences. Cambridge: Harvard College, 2007. Available at http://www.fas.harvard.edu/~secfas/General_Education_Final_Report.pdf (last accessed April 2010).

Reuben, Julie A. *The Making of the Modern University: Intellectual Transformation and the Marginalization of Morality.* Chicago: University of Chicago Press, 1996.

Roche, Mark William. *The Intellectual Appeal of Catholicism and the Idea of a Catholic University.* Notre Dame, IN: University of Notre Dame Press, 2003.

———. *Why Literature Matters in the 21st Century.* New Haven: Yale University Press, 2004.

Rousseau, Jean-Jacques. *Emile, or On Education.* Trans. Allan Bloom. New York: Basic Books, 1979.

Rubin, Harriet. "C.E.O. Libraries Reveal Keys to Success." *New York Times* 21 July 2007: C1.

Rudolph, Frederick. *Curriculum: A History of the American Undergraduate Course of Study since 1636.* San Francisco: Jossey-Bass, 1977.

Ruscio, Kenneth P. "The Distinctive Scholarship of the Selective Liberal Arts College." *Journal of Higher Education* 58 (1987): 205–22.

Saenz, Victor B., and Douglas S. Barrera. *Findings from the 2005 College Student Survey (CSS): National Aggregates.* University of California, Los Angeles: Higher Education Research Institute, 2007. Available at http://www.gseis.ucla.edu/heri/PDFs/2005_CSS_REPORT_FINAL.pdf (last accessed April 2010).

Said, Edward W. *Representations of the Intellectual: The 1993 Reith Lectures.* New York: Vintage, 1996.

Schiller, Friedrich. *On the Aesthetic Education of Man in a Series of Letters.* Trans. Elizabeth M. Wilkinson and L. A. Willoughby. Oxford: Clarendon, 1967.

———. "Was heißt und zu welchem Ende studiert man Universalgeschichte." *Sämtliche Werke.* Münich: Hanser, 2004. 4: 749–67.

Schneider, Carol Geary and Robert Schoenberg. "Contemporary Understandings of Liberal Education." Washington, DC: Association of American Colleges and Universities, 1998.

Schopenhauer, Arthur. "Ueber Sprache und Worte." *Werke in zehn Bänden.* Zürich: Diogenes, 1977. 10: 614–30.

Schwehn, Mark R. *Exiles from Eden: Religion and the Academic Vocation in America.* New York: Oxford University Press, 1993.

Sen, Amartya. *Commodities and Capabilities.* New York: Elsevier, 1985.

Sennett, Richard. *The Corrosion of Character: The Personal Consequences of Work in the New Capitalism.* New York: Norton, 1998.

Shapiro, Harold T. *A Larger Sense of Purpose: Higher Education and Society.* Princeton: Princeton University Press, 2005.

Shorris, Earl. *New American Blues: A Journey through Poverty to Discovery.* New York: Norton, 1997.

Sorcinelli, Mary Deane. "Research Findings on the Seven Principles." *New Directions for Teaching and Learning* 47 (1991): 13–25.

The Spiritual Life of College Students: A National Study of Students' Search for Meaning and Purpose. University of California, Los Angeles: Higher Education Research Institute, n.d. Available at http://www.spirituality.ucla.edu/docs/reports/Spiritual_Life_College_Students_Full_Report.pdf (last accessed April 2010).

Spirituality and the Professoriate: A National Study of Faculty Beliefs, Attitudes, and Behaviors. University of California, Los Angeles: Higher Education Research Institute, n.d. Available at http://www.spirituality.ucla.edu/docs/results/faculty/spirit _professoriate.pdf (last accessed April 2010).

Strunk, William, Jr., and E. B. White. *The Elements of Style.* 4th ed. New York: Longman, 2000.

Summers, Lawrence H. "Address of Lawrence H. Summers, President, Harvard University, Cambridge, MA. 21 October 2001. Available at http://www.hks.harvard.edu/fs/lsummer/speeches/ 2001/inauguration.html (last accessed April 2010).

A Test of Leadership. Charting the Future of U.S. Education. A Report of the Commission Appointed by Secretary of Education Margaret Spellings. Washington, DC: U.S. Department of Education, 2006. Available at http://www.ed.gov/about/bdscomm/ list/hiedfuture/reports/final-report.pdf (last accessed April 2010).

Tocqueville, Alexis de. *Democracy in America.* Trans. George Lawrence. New York: Harper, 1966.

To Read or Not to Read: A Question of National Consequence. Research Report #47. Washington, DC: National Endowment for the Arts, 2007.

Trends and Emerging Practices in General Education. Based on a Survey among Members of the Association of American Colleges and Universities. Washington, DC: Hart Research Associates, 2009. Available at http://www.aacu.org/membership/documents/2009 MemberSurvey_Part2.pdf (last accessed April 2010).

Turner, Sarah E., and William G. Bowen. "The Flight from the Arts and Sciences: Trends in Degrees Conferred." *Science* 250 (26 October 1990): 517–521.

United States Army. *Instructions for American Servicemen in Iraq during World War II.* 1943. Chicago: University of Chicago Press, 2007.

Useem, Michael. *Liberal Education and the Corporation: The Hiring and Advancement of College Graduates.* New York: de Gruyter, 1989.

———. "What the Research Shows." In *Educating Managers: Executive Effectiveness through Liberal Learning.* Joseph S. Johnston, Jr. et al. San Francisco: Jossey-Bass, 1986. 70–101.

Van Doren, Mark. *Liberal Education.* 1943. Boston: Beacon, 1959.

Wallace, Andrew G. "Educating Tomorrow's Doctors: The Thing That Really Matters Is That We Care." *Academic Medicine* 72 (1974): 253–58.

Wallace, Lane. "Multicultural Critical Theory. At B-School?" *New York Times* 10 January 2010. Available at http://www.nytimes .com/2010/01/10/business/10mba.html (last accessed April 2010).

Walvoord, Barbara. *Teaching and Learning in College Introductory Religion Courses.* Oxford: Blackwell, 2008.

"Wanted: Liberal Arts Grads." *Fortune* 12 May 1997.

Warren, Kenneth S. "The Humanities in Medical Education." *Annals of Internal Medicine* 101 (1984): 697–701.

Warren, Russell G. *New Links between General Education and Business Careers.* Washington, DC: Association of American Colleges, 1983.

Weber, Max. "Politics as a Vocation." *From Max Weber: Essays in Sociology.* Ed. H. H. Gerth and C. Wright Mills. New York: Oxford University Press, 1946. 77–128.

———. "Science as a Vocation." *From Max Weber: Essays in Sociology.* Ed. H. H. Gerth and C. Wright Mills. New York: Oxford University Press, 1946. 129–56.

Weil, Simone. "Reflections on the Right Use of School Studies with a View to the Love of God." *Waiting for God.* Trans. Emma Craufu. New York: Perennial, 2001. 57–65.

Whitehead, Alfred North. *The Aims of Education and Other Essays.* 1929. New York: Free Press, 1967.

Winter, David G., David G. McClelland, and Abigail J. Stewart. *A New Case for the Liberal Arts: Assessing Institutional Goals and Student Development.* San Francisco: Jossey-Bass, 1982.

Wolniak, Gregory C., Tricia A. Seifert, and Charles F. Blaich. "A Liberal Arts Education Changes Lives: Why Everyone Can and Should Have This Experience." *Liberal Arts Online* 4.3 (March 2004). Available at http://www.liberalarts.wabash.edu/ lao-4-3-liberal-art-experience/ (last accessed April 2010).

Wuthnow, Robert. *God and Mammon in America.* New York: Macmillan, 1994.